Davis W. Clark

From a Cloud of Witnesses

Vol. 1

Davis W. Clark

From a Cloud of Witnesses
Vol. 1

ISBN/EAN: 9783337341466

Printed in Europe, USA, Canada, Australia, Japan

Cover: Foto ©Thomas Meinert / pixelio.de

More available books at **www.hansebooks.com**

From
A Cloud
Of Witnesses.

Three Hundred and Nine Tributes
to the ~~~~

DAVIS WASGATT CLARK.

CINCINNATI: CURTS & JENNINGS.
NEW YORK: EATON & MAINS.
1897.

CONTENTS.

PUBLISHERS' ANNOUNCEMENT, ... 5
INTRODUCTION, ... 9
TRIBUTES, { Part I.
            { Part II.
INDEXES:
    General, ... 179
    Topical, ... 186
    By Professions, ... 188
    By Nationality, ... 190
APPENDIX
    The International Bible Lesson System: Origin and Extent to Which Used, ... 193
    The Bible Societies and Bible Distribution, ... 196
    Ignorance Respecting the Bible, . . 198
    The Bible as a Text-book, ... 205
    A Laureate's Debt to the Bible, . . 214
    A Prayer Over the Bible, ... 215
    Annotations, ... 217

THE Bible is the life-thought of the world. It is replete with all that can excite the fancy or give wings to the imagination; all that can refine the taste, ennoble the affections, and enlarge the intellect; all, in fine, that can call forth the sublimest thoughts, present the grandest motives of action, and enkindle the loftiest expectation in the illimitable future. It enters into all thought and all feeling, and is allied to all interests, earthly and heavenly. It is just such a book as must be read, will be read. It will travel through all lands, dwell among all people, find a home in all languages, permeate all thought. The very study and effort to destroy it will only cause it to penetrate still more deeply into the world's thought, and imbed it still more firmly in the literature of all ages.

—*BISHOP DAVIS W. CLARK.*
1812–1871.

THIS is the richest compilation of its kind that has yet appeared. It outnumbers by some two hundred quotations the largest collection now in print. It is unique in plan. Its value is enhanced by an introduction, appendix, and quadruple cross index. It shows at a glance how many brilliant thinkers have reflected upon the Bible, and the substance of their thoughts in pithy sentences. The chronological notations of year of birth and death indicate the era to which each belongs. The indexes by nationality and profession serve to locate authorities still more perfectly. The topical index is in itself very suggestive. A metropolitan newspaper recently affirmed editorially that good books concerning the Bible are increasingly in demand. It is believed that this uncommon volume will find a welcome and serve a purpose.

C. & J.

THE Bible is either the most adventurous and astounding fraud that has ever gained currency among men, or the most sublime and momentous system of verities that has at any time appeared upon earth. If the former, it ought not to be impossible to expose the imposture; if the latter, it ought to be possible to command for it the respect of unprejudiced reason and the acceptance of rational faith. That after so many ages it is still in debate, might, to a superficial observer, seem to be to the discredit of its claim. A more astute and careful judge would find the explanation to consist, in part, of the unique nature and intrinsic difficulty of the claim itself, and, in part, of the peculiar relations of the jury to the question in dispute.
—*BISHOP RANDOLPH S. FOSTER.*

INTRODUCTION.

THIS compilation is not intended to encourage bibliolatry. The Bible is God's vehicle. By it he comes to our minds and hearts. To worship the vehicle is idolatrous. If the book could speak, it would cry as the angel did to John, "See thou do it not!"

The trend of our day, however, is not in the direction of over-veneration for the Bible. The first effect of the application of the scientific method to the Scriptures is to mar their beauty for the average eye. At first blush they are left without form or comeliness, as the Messiah himself appeared.

A prince of the American pulpit once exclaimed, "These scientists and higher critics are God's Irishmen: with pick, spade, and barrow, they are removing the *débris* of tradition. After their work is all done, the *rock* will still remain."

Some timid souls, however, may think the pick is striking deeper than the superimposed strata of human opinion. They may even imagine that the rock itself is being drilled preparatory to the introduction of explosives that, when the mine is sprung, will leave nothing of it.

While the case is still pending, this cloud of witnesses has been summoned. It is a surprising array, representative of every nation, profession, rank, and station; of every faith, unfaith, anti-faith. The testimony is clear and largely disinterested. While its power is certainly cumulative, it is not expected or claimed to be conclusive. It will probably be generally conceded, however, that it establishes a good and unique character for the Bible. It

Introduction.

justifies at least a suspension of opinion until the case of the Scientific Method *versus* the Bible is closed and the *book* (not *a priori* theories concerning it) is vindicated, as it certainly will be.

In these noble tributes, culled with care from every available source, many will find expression of the profoundest sentiments of their souls concerning the Bible. Admiration, reverence, love, faith, here have a vocabulary.

TRIBUTES
PART 1.

*M*AY we not discover in the fortunes of this perhaps latest of all the sacred writers* save John, a significent type of the fortunes of that inspired Word on which we have been dwelling? Ofttimes has it been dragged over the sharp rocks of hostile criticism, ofttimes across the hot sands of scorching sarcasm, ofttimes through the mire of filthy jesting; but God has been with it. It refuses to die. Even when its enemies have fancied it finally and forever dispatched, it has erelong reasserted its indestructible vitality, overtoppling earthborn fanes of superstition, and replacing them with temples not made with hands. Even the works of nature are frail, caducous, and transitory when compared with this inspired Book. The grass withereth, the flower fadeth, but the Word of our God abideth forever.
—PRESIDENT WILLIAM F. WARREN.

---

* *Tradition says effort to martyr St. Mark, by dragging him behind a chariot, failed.*

A Cloud of Witnesses.

Part I.

1 TO the Bible men will return because they can not do without it; because happiness is our being's end and aim, and happiness belongs to righteousness, and righteousness is revealed in the Bible. For this simple reason men will return to the Bible, just as a man who tried to give up food, thinking it was a vain thing and that he could do without it, would return to food; or a man who tried to give up sleep, thinking it was a vain thing and he could do without it, would return to sleep.

 1822-1888. —MATTHEW ARNOLD.

2 ALL Scripture is practical, and intended to minister to our improvement rather than to our curiosity. —*Ibid.*

3 IT is astonishing how a Bible sentence clinches and sums up an argument. —*Ibid.*

4 THERE is no passion that is not finely expressed in those parts of the inspired writings which are proper for Divine songs and anthems.
    1672–1719.   —JOSEPH ADDISON.

5 THE Scripture so speaketh that, with the height of it, it laughs proud and lofty-spirited men to scorn; with the depth of it, it terrifies those who, with attention, look into it; with the truth of it, it feeds men of the greatest knowledge and understanding; and with the sweetness of it, it nourisheth babes and sucklings.
    354–430.   —ST. AUGUSTINE,
                  Bishop of Hippo.

6 I HAVE examined all, as well as my narrow sphere, my straitened means, and my busy life would allow me; and the result is, that the Bible is the best book in the world. 1735–1826. —JOHN ADAMS,
    Second President United States.

7 SO great is my veneration for the Bible that the earlier my children begin to read it, the more confident will be my hopes that they will prove useful citizens to their country and respectable members of society.
 1767-1848. —JOHN QUINCY ADAMS,
   6th President United States.

8 IN what light soever we regard the Bible, whether with reference to revelation, to history, or to morality, it is an invaluable mine of knowledge and virtue.   *—Ibid.*

9 I SPEAK as a man of the world to men of the world; and I say to you, "Search the Scriptures." The Bible is the Book of all others to be read at all ages and in all conditions of human life; not to be read once or twice or thrice through, and then laid aside, but to be read in small portions of one or two chapters every day, and never to be intermitted unless by some overruling necessity.
     —Ibid.

10 SIRS, I have devoured it [the Bible],
finding in it words suitable to,
and descriptive of, the states of my
mind. The Lord, by his Divine Spirit,
has been pleased to give me an understanding of what I read therein.
  1777–1825. —ALEXANDER I,
       Czar of Russia.

11 NO man ever did or ever can become truly eloquent without being a constant reader of the Bible,
and an admirer of its purity and sublimity. —FISHER AMES.
  1756–1808.

12 BEFORE me lay the Sacred Text:
The help, the guide, the balm of
souls perplexed.
 1538–83. —ALEXANDER ARBUTHNOT.

13 ACCEPT the glad tidings,
 The warnings and chidings,
Found in this volume of heavenly
 lore;
With faith that's unfailing,
And love all prevailing,
Trust in its promise of life evermore. —*Anon.*

14 THE Bible is full and complete as a book of direction; human life is full and complete as a field of exercise.
1835—— —Lyman Abbott.

15 AS a mere book it will never die. Such height of thought, such breadth of expression, such aptness in speaking to the great heart of the race,—surely it will live and be read in the world's latest afternoon; and when the last ray is fading out of the eye of humanity, it will not be toward Homer or Plato that the straining orb will be found directing itself, but rather toward the various glories of that one Book which deserves to be called the Book of Mankind.
—*Ad Fidem.* (F. E. Burr.)

16 THEY who are not induced to believe and live as they ought by those discoveries which God hath made in Scripture, would stand out against any evidence whatever, even that of a messenger sent express from the other world.
1662-1732. —Francis Atterbury.

17 A SACRED ark, which from the deeps
  Garners the life for worlds to be,
And with its precious burden sweeps
  Adown dark Time's destroying sea. —*Anon.*

18 OF most other things it may be said, "Vanity of vanities, all is vanity;" but of the Scriptures, Verity of verities, all is verity.
—JOHN ARROWSMITH, d. 1659.

19 THE Bible evidently transcends all human effort; it has upon its face the impress of divinity; it shines with a light which, from its clearness and its splendor, shows itself to be celestial. Surely, then, it is the Word of God. —ARCHIBALD ALEXANDER. 1772-1851.

20 THE Bible is the standard for earth's erring millions. The sacred rays of Love, Peace, Truth, and Purity beam and radiate from its glowing page. —*Anon.*

21 THE Bible is the only cement of nations.
—Christian Karl Josias von Bunsen.
1791–1860.   (Chevalier Bunsen.)

22 THERE is not a book on earth so favorable to all the kind, and to all the sublime affections, or so unfriendly to hatred and persecution, to tyranny, injustice, and every sort of malevolence, as the Gospel.
1735–1803.   —James Beattie.

23 NO book in the world equals the Scripture, even as regards the manners and affections.—*Bengel on Acts xx, 37.*
—Johann Albrecht Bengel.
1687–1752.

24 WE think of the Bible as of a structure solid and eternal.
—Cyrus Augustus Bartol.
1813——

25 'TIS very vain for me to boast
How small a price this Bible cost;
The day of judgment will make clear
'T was very cheap or very dear.
1746–1767.   —Michael Bruce,
[On the fly-leaf of his Bible.]

26 SO FAR as I have observed God's dealings with my soul, the flights of preachers sometimes entertained me; but it was Scripture expressions which did penetrate my heart, and in a way peculiar to themselves.

1722–1787. —J. BROWN,
Of Haddington.

27 THE Bible is a precious storehouse and the Magna Charta of a Christian. There he reads of his Heavenly Father's love and of his dying Savior's legacies. There he sees a map of his travels through the wilderness, and a landscape, too, of Canaan.

—BERRIDGE.

28 IF these facts (on the origin, nature, and progress of the Christian religion) are not therefore established, nothing in the history of mankind can be believed.

d. 1843.
—RT. HON. SIR C. KENDAL BUSHE,
Chief Justice.

29 THE Bible owes its continued authority and influence to the fact that it *really contains* the Word of God; that in its various records flows down the full and vigorous river of God's truth and grace, in the history of a race peculiarly and providentially fitted to receive special communications from on high. Nothing can ever change or destroy the sublime merits and religious influence of the Mosaic dispensation; nothing outlive the strains of David's glorious harp; nothing take the place of Isaiah's exalted prophecies; much less can the record of our Savior's life and conversations ever cease to win the profoundest reverence and gratitude of mankind. —Henry W. Bellows. 1814-1882.

30 ALTHOUGH the Greek literature of the New Testament has no Demosthenes "On the Crown" or Plato's Republic, as it has no Iliad or Prometheus, yet it lays the foundation of the sermon and the theological tract, those forms of literature which,

however little they may appeal to the æsthetic taste, have yet been the literary means of a world-transforming power, as, from pulpit and chair, Christian ministers have stirred the hearts and minds of mankind.

1841—— —CHARLES A. BRIGGS, Lecture: Languages of the Bible. God's Word Man's Light and Guide. Lectures before N. Y. S. S. Association, American Tract Society.

31 I FIND the Bible the patriot's chart-book, the child's delight, the old man's comfort, the young man's guide. In its pages the sick and the weary find solace, and the dying hope and peace. —RICHARD BEARD. 1799-1880.

32 THE poetry of the Bible has been the forming-power of the greatest modern poems. —*Ibid.*

33 THE Bible stands alone in human literature in its elevated conception of manhood as to character and conduct. It is the invaluable training-book of the world.

1813-1887. —HENRY WARD BEECHER.

34 THE Bible emptied, effete, worn out! If all the wisest men of the world were placed man to man, they could not sound the shallowest depths of the Gospel of John. —*Ibid.*

35 WHOEVER made that book made me. It knows all that is in my heart. It tells me what no one else except God can know about me. Whoever made me, wrote that book.
—BISHOP BOONE'S Chinese Assistant in the translation of the Bible (before his conversion).

36 I BELIEVE the Bible, all of it! The very things I do n't understand I believe the most of all. I would n't exchange my faith for any man's knowledge.
1818–1885. —HENRY W. SHAW, (Josh Billings.)

37 THERE never was found in any age of the world either religion or law that did so highly exalt the public good as the Bible.
1561–1626. —FRANCIS BACON.

38 AS THE moon, for all those darker parts we call her spots, gives us much greater light than the stars, which seem all luminous, so will the Scripture; for all its obscurer passages afford more light than the brightest human authors.

1626–1691.   —ROBERT BOYLE.

39 AS SOME pictures seem to have their eyes fixed upon every one from whatsoever part of the room he eyes them, there is scarce a frame of spirit a man can be of, to which some passage of Scripture is not as applicable as if it were meant for or said to him.   —*Ibid.*

40 I USE the Scriptures, not as an arsenal to be resorted to only for arms and weapons, . . . but as a matchless temple, where I delight to contemplate the beauty, the symmetry, and the magnificence of the structure, and to increase my awe and excite my devotion to the Deity there preached and adored. —*Ibid.*

41 THOUGH many other books are comparable to cloth, in which by a small pattern we may safely judge of the whole piece, yet the Bible is like a fair suit of arras, of which though a shred may assure you of the fineness of the colors and richness of the stuff, yet the hangings never appear to their full advantage but when they are displayed to their full dimensions and are seen together.
—*Ibid.*

42 IN THE Bible the ignorant may learn all required knowledge, and the most knowing may learn to discern their ignorance. —*Ibid.*

43 THE Parable of the Prodigal Son, the most beautiful fiction that ever was invented; our Savior's speech to his disciples, with which he closed his earthly ministrations, full of the sublimest dignity and tenderest affection, surpass anything that I ever read, and, like the spirit by which they were dictated, fly directly to the heart. —WILLIAM COWPER.
1731–1800.

44 'TIS Revelation satisfies all doubts,
　　Explains all mysteries, except her own,
And so illuminates the path of life,
That fools discover it and stray no more. —*Ibid.*

45 A CRITIC on the Sacred Book should be
Candid and learned, dispassionate and free,—
Free from the wayward bias bigots feel,
From fancy's influence and intemperate zeal. —*Ibid.*

46 NO other Scriptures of man compare with it for wide, deep, and ever-growing influence. It is the highest work of its class—that is, of *the sacred writings of mankind*—and these *sacred writings* are, among all other writings, the most important and influential. . . .

Every commanding race, every vast civilization, has been directed and controlled by its sacred writings. The hundred and fifty millions of Hindus have been ruled, during twenty-five centuries, by their Vedas and Puranas. Chinese civilization has taken its stamp from the "Four Books" and "The Kings." The brilliant career of the Persian Empire was inspired throughout by the Zend-Avesta. The tribes of Arabia were gathered, molded, banded, and wielded in a resistless tide of conquest by the Koran. The sacred books of the Buddhists have been the leaven of civilization among a third part of the human race during a vast period of time. If we judge them by their influence, these are the great books of the human race. But, for various reasons, the Bible stands above them all. The others are the books of particular races — of the Hindus only, or the Mongols, or the Persians, or the Chinese; but the Bible has a constituency composed of all the races of the world. The others belong to decaying, arrested, or dead civilizations; the Bible to the advancing and all-conquering races, who stand for the highest civilization attained on this planet. The others are either narrow or shallow in some directions; the Bible is a fountain whose waters feed intellect, heart, life, promoting the highest worship as well as the largest humanity. . . .

Kingdoms fall, institutions perish, civilizations change, human doctrines disappear; but the imperishable truths which pervade and sanctify the Bible shall bear it up above the flood of change and the deluge of years.
—James Freeman Clark,
Lecture: "What is the Bible? and Where Did it Come From?"
1810–1883.

47 THE incongruity of the Bible, with the age of its birth, its freedom from earthly mixtures, its original unborrowed, solitary greatness, the suddenness with which it broke forth amidst the universal gloom,—these to me are strong indications of its divine descent. I can not reconcile them with a human origin.
—William Ellery Channing.
1780–1842.

48 THE Gospels, in which the Christ is placed before us so vividly, are, in truth, the chief repositories of divine wisdom. The greatest productions of human genius have little quickening power in comparison with these simple narratives. In reading the Gospels, I feel myself in presence of one who speaks as man never spake; whose voice is not of the earth; who speaks with a tone of reality and authority altogether his own. . . . No books astonish me like the Gospels. . . . Of all books they deserve most the study of youth and age. —*Ibid.*

49 IN the Bible there is more that *finds* me than I have experienced in all other books put together; the words of the Bible find me at greater depths of my being; and whatever *finds* me brings with it an irresistible evidence of its having proceeded from the Holy Spirit.

—SAMUEL TAYLOR COLERIDGE,
In Confessions of an Inquiring Spirit: London Ed., William Pickering. 1840.
1772-1834.

50 INTENSE study of the Bible will keep any man from being vulgar in point of style. —*Ibid.*

51 WOULD I withhold the Bible from the cottager or the artisan? Heaven forbid! The fairest flower that ever clomb up a cottage window is not so fair a sight to my eyes as the Bible gleaming through the lower panes. —*Ibid,, p. 85.*

52 FOR more than a thousand years the Bible, collectively taken, has gone hand in hand with civilization, science, law; in short, with moral and intellectual cultivation; always supporting, and often leading, the way. —*Ibid., p. 71.*

53 THE sanctions of the Divine law cover the whole area of human action, reach every case, punish every sin, and recompense every virtue.

Its rewards and its punishments are graduated with perfect justice.

 1769-1828. —DeWitt Clinton.

54 THERE was plainly wanting a Divine revelation to recover mankind out of their universal corruption and degeneracy.

 1675-1729. —Samuel Clarke.

55 IT is just as if the art of ship-building should be conducted without helms. Tall ships should be set afloat to be guilded by the winds only. For such are the immortal ships on the sea of human life without the Bible. Its knowledge, its principles, ought from the first to be as much a part of the educated, intelligent constitution as the keel or rudder is part and parcel of a well-built ship.

 1807—— —George B. Cheever,
  Pilgrim of the Jungfrau, p. 59.

56 I CAN not look around me without being struck by the analogy observable in the works of God. I find the

Bible written in the style of his other books of creation and providence. The pen seems in the same hand. I see it at times, indeed, write mysteriously in each of these books; but I know that mystery in the works of God is only another name for my ignorance. The moment, therefore, that I become humble, all becomes right. —RICHARD CECIL.
1748–1810.

57 THE Bible resembles an extensive garden where there is a vast variety and profusion of fruits and flowers, some of which are more essential or more splendid than others; but there is not a blade suffered to grow in it which has not its use and beauty in the system. —*Ibid.*

58 I EARNESTLY hope that God's day may be hallowed, and his Word may be studied through this whole land, till their obligations are felt and acknowledged by all its people.
1782–1866.   —LEWIS CASS.

59 I HAVE but one book, but that is the best.
—WILLIAM COLLINS TO DR. JOHNSON.
1720–1756.

60 A NOBLE Book! All men's Book! It is our first oldest statement of the never-ending problem—man's destiny and God's ways with him here on earth; and all in such free-flowing outlines—grand in its sincerity, in its simplicity and its epic melody.
1795–1881. —THOMAS CARLYLE.

61 IN the poorest cottage are books—is one Book wherein, for several thousands of years, the spirit of man has found light and nourishment and an interpreting response to whatever is deepest in him. —*Ibid.*

62 TO see God's own law universally acknowledged as it stands in the Holy Written Book; to see this—or the true unwearied aim and struggle toward this—is a thing worth living and dying for. —*Ibid.*

63 WHEN one said to Carlyle that there was nothing remarkable in the Book of Proverbs, he simply replied, "Make a few."

64 WHATEVER strong situations I have in my tales are not of my creation, but are taken from the Bible.
—THOMAS HENRY HALL CAINE.
1853-

65 THE Bible is unquestionably the richest repository of thought and imagery, and the best model of pure style that our language can boast.
—W. B. CLULOW.

66 SCHOLARS may quote Plato in studies, but the hearts of millions shall quote the Bible at their daily toil, and draw strength from its inspiration as the meadows draw it from the brook.
—MONCURE DANIEL CONWAY.
1832-

67 OR whether more abstractedly we look
  Or on the writers or the written book,
  Whence but for heaven could men unskilled in arts,
  In several ages born, in several parts
  Weave such agreeing truths? or how or why
  Should all conspire to cheat us with a lie?
  Unasked their pains, ungrateful their advice;
  Starving their gain, and martydom their price. —JOHN DRYDEN.
  1631-1700.

68 FOR Scripture style is noble and divine,
  It speaks no less than God in every line;
  It is not built on disquisition vain,
  The things we must believe are few and plain. —*Ibid.*

69 BIBLE Christianity is the companion of liberty in all its conflicts, the cradle of its infancy, and the divine source of its claims.
    —CHARLES HENRI CLEREL DE
1805-1859.   TOCQUEVILLE.

70 THE Bible is a window in the prison of hope through which we look into eternity. —TIMOTHY DWIGHT.
1752-1818.

71 THE grand old Book of God still stands; and this old earth, the more its leaves are turned over and pondered, the more it will sustain and illustrate the Sacred Word.
1813-1895. —JAMES DWIGHT DANA.

72 THE first thought that strikes the scientific reader is the evidence of divinity, not merely in the first verse of the record and the successive fiats, but in the whole order of creation. There is so much that the most recent readings of science have for the first time explained, that the idea of man as the author becomes utterly in

comprehensible. By proving the record true, science pronounces it divine; for who could have correctly narrated the secrets of eternity but God himself? —*Ibid.*

73 AND, finally, I may state, as the conclusion of the whole matter, that the Bible contains within itself all that, under God, is required to account for and dispose of all forms of infidelity, and to turn to the best and highest uses all that man can learn of nature.
—Chancellor Dawson.

74 NO better lessons than those of the Bible can I teach my child.
1713–1784.   —Denis Diderot.

75 THE cruel battles fought some years ago round the Malakoff tower showed that in that fortress lay the key of war, and on it depended defeat or triumph. So the multiplied attacks directed in our day against the Bible indicate that it is, in view of

our adversaries, the tower which, above all others, must be torn down.
—Jean Henri Merle, D'Aubigne.
1794–1872.

76 THE voice of the past is now seldom heard in the din of clashing opinions and interests. Saint Augustine and Saint Chrysostom, of the early Christian era, commanded the attention of the world. The schoolmen of the Dark Ages led the thought of the times through universities, where thirty thousand students were entered on the rolls. Luther and Melanchthon, and Erasmus and Grotius, were spokesmen of the effort for spiritual, intellectual, and civil liberty, which has incalculably affected the destinies of mankind. The Puritan divines of the first hundred years of New England settlement inspired the thought and governed the course of the colleges and controlled the minds of the people. Now, no one, outside the antiquaries and critical few, reads the Fathers of the Church, the Schoolmen, the Leaders

of the Reformation, or Cotton Mather, or Jonathan Edwards. The body of truth from which they derived their doctrines and constructed their systems is found in the open Bible, by every fireside in the land. From its pages the individual, according to his or her light and opportunity, draws the lessons of life.

 1834- —CHAUNCEY M. DEPEW.

77 THE next point to be attended to is this: What books ought you to read? There are some books that are absolutely indispensable to the kind of education that we are contemplating, and to the profession that we are considering; and of all these the most indispensable, the most useful, the one whose knowledge is most effective, is the Bible. There is no book from which more valuable lessons can be learned. I am considering it now not as a religious book, but as a manual of utility, of professional preparation and professional use, for a journalist. There is, perhaps, no book whose style is more suggestive and more

instructive, from which you learn more directly that sublime simplicity which never exaggerates, which recounts the greatest event, with solemnity of course, but without sentimentality or affectation; none which you open with such confidence and lay down with such reverence; there is no book like the Bible. When you get into a controversy and want exactly the right answer, when you are looking for an expression, what is there that closes a dispute like a verse from the Bible? What is it that sets up the right principle for you, which pleads for a policy, for a cause, so much as the right passage of Holy Scripture?
—CHARLES A. DANA,
Of the *New York Sun*, in "Journalism," a lecture at Union College.
1819—

78 IN this Book is all the wisdom of the world.
—GEORG HENRICH AUGUST EWALD,
In conversation with Dean Stanley.
1803-1875.

79 OUT from the heart of nature rolled
The burdens of the Bible old.
—RALPH WALDO EMERSON.
1803–1882.

80 THERE is yet another sword to be delivered to me. I mean the sacred Bible, which is the Sword of the Spirit, without which we are nothing, neither can we do anything.
—EDWARD VI,
(At his coronation, on receiving the swords of England, France, and Ireland.)
Reigned 1547–1553.

81 ALL the distinctive features and superiority of our republican institutions are derived from the teachings of Scripture. —EDWARD EVERETT.
1794–1865.

82 THIS narrative contains nothing which does not accurately correspond to a court of Pharaoh in the best times of the kingdom.
1837— —GEORG EBERS.

83   GOD has not so poised the Rock of Ages that the higher or lower criticism, with pickax or crowbar digging out a chronological inaccuracy here or prying off a historical contradiction there, is going to upset it. The critic may be all right, and the crowbar may be all right; but the Rock of Ages is all right too, and it will stand forever.
—Professor L. J. Evans.
Biblical Scholarship and Inspiration, p. 70

84   THE yardstick, if used for microscopic measurements, would fail; but as a yardstick it is infallible. So with the Bible. Its infallibility is not microscopic, infinitesimal infallibility respecting all particular things in the heavens above and the earth beneath, or in the waters under the earth. —*Ibid., p.* 831.

85   IS it not the claim and glory of the Gospel story that it combines the dignity and authority of a heavenly

recital with the piquant frankness of the conversational fireside tale?
       —*Ibid.*

86 WHICH book has done the most for liberty, justice, progress? Which book has most persistently branded, defied, and theatened every form of tyranny? Which book has spoken with the truest pathos to the wounded and sorrowing heart? The test is fair; the words and works are before you—judge them.
  —*Ecce Deus:* JOSEPH PARKER.

87 YOUNG man, my advice to you is, that you cultivate an acquaintance with, and a firm belief in, the Holy Scriptures. This is your certain interest.
 1706-1790. —BENJAMIN FRANKLIN.

88 A BIBLE and a newspaper in every house, a good school in every district—all studied and appreciated as they merit—are the principal support of virtue, morality, and civil liberty.
       —*Ibid.*

89 THE Scriptures teach us the best way of living, the noblest way of suffering, and the most comfortable way of dying. —JOHN FLAVEL. 1630–1691.

90 HOW precious is the Book divine,
By inspiration given!
Bright as a lamp its doctrines shine,
To guide our souls to heaven.
1739–1819. —JOHN FAWCETT.

91 I WOULD not now exchange for any amount of money the acquaintance with the Bible that was drummed into me when a boy. —EUGENE FIELD. 1850–1895.

92 THE uncommon beauty and marvelous English of the Protestant Bible—it lives on the ear like music that never can be forgotten; like the sound of choice bells which the convert hardly knows how to forego. Its felicities often seem to be things rather than mere words. It is part of

the national mind, and the anchor of national seriousness.
  —Frederick William Faber.
    1814–1863.

93 THE peculiar genius, if such a word may be permitted, which breathes through it [the authorized version]; the mingled tenderness and majesty; the Saxon simplicity, the preternatural grandeur, unequaled, unapproached in the attempted improvements of modern scholars,—all are here, and bear the impress of the mind of one man, and that man William Tyndale.
  —James Anthony Froude.
    1818–1894.

94 THE Bible—a stream, where alike the elephant may swim and the lamb may wade.
  —Pope Gregory I: The Great.
    544–604.

95 OTHER books, after shining their season, may perish in flames fiercer than those which consumed the Alexandrian library. This, in

essence, must remain pure as gold and unconsumable as asbestos.

 1813-1878. —George Gilfillan.

96 IT has been subjected, along with many others books, to the fire of the keenest investigation — a fire which has contemptuously burned up the cosmogony of the Shaster, the absurd fables of the Koran; nay, the husbandry of the Georgics, the historical truth of Livy, the artistic merit of many a popular poem, the authority of many a book of philosophy and science. And yet there this artless, loosely-piled book lies unhurt, untouched, with not one page singed; and not even the smell of fire has passed upon it. —*Ibid.*

97 I BELIEVE in God, and adore him. I have a firm belief in the history contained in the Old and New Testaments and in the regeneration of the human race by the sacrifice of Jesus Christ. I bow before the mysteries of the Bible and the gospel, and I hold myself aloof from scientific

discussion and solutions by which men have attempted to explain them.
—FRANCOIS PIERRE GUILLAUME GUIZOT. 1787-1874.

98 HOLD fast to the Bible as the sheet-anchor to your liberties, write its precepts in your hearts, and practice them in your lives. To the influence of this Book we are indebted for all progress made in our true civilization, and to this we must look as our guide in the future. —U. S. GRANT, 18th President U. S. 1822-1885.

99 THIS is the cannon (the Bible) that will make Italy free.
1807-1882. —GIUSEPPE GARIBALDI.

100 WE all require to feed in the pastures and to drink at the wells of Holy Scripture.
—WILLIAM EWART GLADSTONE. 1809—

101 IF I am asked what is the remedy for the deeper sorrows of the human heart—what a man should chiefly

look to in his progress through life as the power that is to sustain him under trials and enable him manfully to confront his afflictions—I must point to something which in a well-known hymn is called "The old, old story," told of an old, old Book, and taught with an old, old teaching, which is the greatest and best gift ever given to mankind. —*Ibid.*

102 IT is impossible to mentally or socially enslave a Bible-reading people. The principles of the Bible are the ground-work of human freedom.
1811–1872. —Horace Greeley.

103 NO criticism will be able to perplex the confidence I have entertained in a writing whose contents have stirred up and given life to my energy by its own.
—Johann Wolfgang von Goethe.
1749–1833.

104 IT is a belief in the Bible, the fruits of deep meditation, which has served me as the guide of my moral

and literary life. I have found it a capital safely invested, and richly productive of interest. *—Ibid.*

105 I ESTEEM the Gospels to be thoroughly genuine, for there shines forth from them the reflected splendor of a sublimity proceeding from the person of Jesus Christ of so divine a kind as only the divine could have manifested upon earth. *—Ibid.*

106 THE farther the ages advance in cultivation, the more can the Bible be used, partly as the foundation, partly as the means of education, not, of course, by superficial, but by really wise men. *—Ibid.*

107 IT is a sacred duty to hear and devoutly read the Word of God.
—Cardinal Gibbons,
In sermon in Cathedral at Baltimore. 1834—

108 WHATEVER changes we may expect to be introduced by new discoveries, in our present view of

the universe and the globe the prominent traits of this vast picture will remain. And these only are traced out in this admirable account of Genesis. These outlines were sufficient for the moral purposes of the book; the scientific details are for us patiently to investigate. They were, no doubt, unknown to Moses, as the details of the life and of the work of the Savior were unknown to the great prophets who announced his coming, and traced out with master hand his character and objects, centuries before his appearance on earth. But the same divine hand which lifted up before the eyes of Daniel and of Isaiah the veil which covered the tableau of the time to come, unveiled before the eyes of the author of Genesis the earliest ages of creation. And Moses was the prophet of the past, as Daniel and Isaiah and many others were the prophets of the future. —ARNOLD HENRY GUYOT.
1807-1884.

109 TO say that the Hebrew literature is the best literature that the world has ever produced is to say very little. It is separated widely from all other sacred writings. Its constructive ideas are as far above those of the other books of religion as the heavens are above the earth. I pity the man who has had the Bible in his hand from his infancy, and who has learned in his maturer years something of the literature of the other religions, but who now needs to have this statement verified.
—WASHINGTON GLADDEN,
"Who Wrote the Bible?" p. 15.

110 BIBLES laid open—millions of surprises!   GEORGE HERBERT.
1593–1632.

111 THIS Book of stars lights to eternal bliss.   —*Ibid.*

112 THE Bible is common sense inspired.   —R. HOWELLS.

113 SYSTEMATIC study of the Sacred Scriptures is essential to the promotion of a spiritual life.
    1802–1887. —MARK HOPKINS.

114 EVERY leaf is a spacious plain, every line a flowing brook, every period a lofty mountain.
    1714–1758. —JAMES HERVEY.

115 THE Bible is the most sensible book in the world. The maiden does not find her chapter in the Bible from which she passes away when she comes among mothers, to find her new section ready for her; but the whole Bible is the common heritage of mother and maiden. —JOHN HALL.
    1829—

116 THE Word of God is solid; it will stand a thousand readings; and the man who has gone over it the most frequently and carefully is the surest of finding new wonders there.
    1814–1867. —JAMES HAMILTON.

117 IN preparing a guide to immortality, infinite wisdom gave not a dictionary nor a grammar, but a Bible—a Book which, in trying to catch the heart of man, should captivate his taste, and which, in transforming his affections, should also expand his intellect. —*Ibid.*

118 THE most illiterate Christian, if he can but read his English Bible, will not only attain all that practical knowledge which is essential to salvation, but, by God's blessing, he will become learned in everything relating to his religion.
— SAMUEL HORSLEY.
1733–1806.

119 SOME of the pleasantest recollections of my childhood are connected with the voluntary study of an ancient Bible which belonged to my grandmother. I enumerate, as they issue, the childish impressions which come crowding out of the pigeon-holes in my brain, in which

they have lain almost undisturbed for forty years.
—Thomas Henry Huxley.
1825—

120 I HAVE always been strongly in favor of secular education, in the sense of education without theology; but I must confess I have been no less seriously perplexed to know by what practical measures the religious feeling, which is the essential basis of conduct, was to be kept up, in the present utterly chaotic state of opinion on these matters, without the use of the Bible. The pagan moralists lack life and color; and even the noble stoic, Marcus Antoninus, is too high and refined for an ordinary child. Take the Bible as a whole; make the severest deductions which fair criticism can dictate, and there still remains in this old literature a vast residuum of moral beauty and grandeur. By the study of what other book could children be so much humanized? If Bible-reading is not accompanied by constraint and solemnity,

I do not believe there is anything in which children take more pleasure.
—*Ibid.*, in public address.

121 I HOLD to the Bible as a great educator. It is an unquestioned fact that for the last three centuries this Book has been woven into all that is best and noblest in English literature and history. —*Ibid.*

122 FOR fifty years I have been studying the Bible with all my might, digging into it and searching it through and through, and it is always fresh. I seem still to be only scratching the surface.
—Canon Hoare.

123 WE are astonished to find in a lyrical poem, so limited in compass, the whole universe—the heavens and the earth—sketched with a few bold touches.
—Baron William von Humboldt, 1767–1835. On Psalm civ.

124 ALL that has been done to weaken the foundation of an implicit faith in the Bible, as a whole, has been at the expense of the sense of religious obligation, and at the cost of human happiness. —J. G. HOLLAND.
1819–1881.

125 WE believe that the Scriptures of the Old and New Testaments form a collection of laws never to be repealed; of infallible judgments never to be reversed; of answers to the most momentous inquiries man can propose, answers never to be recalled; all the information which heaven deems necessary for earth—so sufficient that no serious doubts can ever be started, no important question ever arise on any moral subject, which it has not anticipated, and to which it does not reply. —JOHN HARRIS.
1667–1719.

126 I SEE that the Bible fits into every fold and crevice of the human heart. I am a man; and I believe

that this is God's Book, because it is man's Book. —HENRY HALLAM.
1777–1859.

127 THERE is scarcely any part of knowledge worthy of the mind of man but from Scripture it may have some direction and light.
1553–1600. —RICHARD HOOKER.

128 WHAT a Book! Vast and wide as the world, rooted in the abysses of Creation, and towering up behind the blue secrets of heaven. Sunrise and sunset, promise and fulfillment, birth and death, the whole drama of humanity, all in this Book!
1797–1847. —HEINRICH HEINE.

129 I ATTRIBUTE my illumination entirely and simply to the reading of a book. Yes, and it is an old, homely book, modest as nature, also as natural as she herself—a book which has a work-a-day and unassuming look, like the sun which warms us, like the bread which nourishes us—a book which looks at us as cordially and

blessingly as the old grandmother who daily reads in it with her dear trembling lips, and with her spectacles on her nose; and this book is called shortly *the* book, the bible. With right is this named the Holy Scripture; he who has lost his God can find him again in this book, and he who has never known him is here struck by the breath of the Divine Word. —*Ibid.*

130 IN a few chosen sentences we acquire more accurate knowledge of the affairs of Egypt, Tyre, Syria, Assyria, Babylon, and other neighboring nations than had been preserved to us in all the other remains of antiquity up to the recent discoveries in hieroglyphical and cuneiform monuments.
—LORD ARTHUR HERVEY,
Smith B. Dic. Vol. III, p. 1561, Am. Ed.

131 IF an uninterested spectator, after a careful perusal of the New Testament, were asked what he conceived to be its distinguishing characteristic,

he would reply without hesitation, "That wonderful spirit of philanthropy by which it is distinguished." It is a perpetual commentary on that eternal aphorism, "God is love."
 1764-1831. —ROBERT HALL.

132 ALL human discoveries seem to be made only for the purpose of confirming more and more strongly the truths contained in the Holy Scriptures.
  — JOHN FREDERICK WILLIAM HERSCHEL.
1792-1871.

133 IN those fragments, there is the triumph of the great Personality of all time. Lord of Life, we call him wisely. Because the Bible incloses the Four Gospels, explains, illustrates, leads down to them and leads back to them; because, so leading, it shows always that life is always master, and that forms obey—forms, methods, law, fashion, and all the outside—that these obey and must obey; because the Bible is the Book of Life, and the Book of the Lord of Life—because of this it keeps its hold upon the world.

1822— —EDWARD EVERETT HALE.

134 GIVE to the people who toil and suffer, for whom this world is hard and bad, the belief that there is a better made for them; scatter the gospel among the villages, a Bible for every cottage.

1802-1885. —VICTOR MARIE HUGO.

135 THEY have the Bible.—John Jay, First Chief Justice U. S., when asked if he had any farewell address to leave his children.

1745-1829.

136 THAT Book is the rock on which the Republic stands.

—ANDREW JACKSON,
1767-1845.   7th President U. S.

137 I HAVE always said, and always will say, that the studious perusal of the Sacred Volume will make better citizens, better fathers, and better husbands.   —THOMAS JEFFERSON,
1743-1826.   3d President U. S.

138 I HAVE carefully and regularly perused the Holy Scriptures, and am of opinion that the volume, independently of its Divine origin, contains more sublimity, purer morality, more important history, and finer strains, both of poetry and eloquence, than could be collected within the same compass from all other books that were ever composed in any age or in any idiom.
 1746-1798. — W. JONES.

139 GOD in tender indulgence to our different dispositions has strewed the Bible with flowers, dignified it with wonders, and enriched it with delight. —F. JOUBERT.
 1689-1763.

140 YOUNG man, attend to the voice of one who has possessed a certain degree of fame, and who will shortly appear before his Maker. Read the Bible every day of your life.
 1709-1784. —SAMUEL JOHNSON,
      IN conversation.

141 CITIES fall, kingdoms come to nothing, empires fade away as smoke. Where is Numa, Minos, Lycurgus? Where are their books, and what is become of their laws? But that this Book no tyrant should have been able to consume, no tradition to choke, no heretic maliciously to corrupt; that it should stand unto this day, amid the wreck of all that is human, without the alteration of one sentence so as to change the doctrine taught therein,—surely there is a very singular providence claiming our attention in a most remarkable manner. —JOHN JEWELL,
1522-1571.   Bishop of Salisbury.

142 LOOK in the Holy Scriptures for truth, not for eloquence, and read them with that mind wherewith they were written—for thine everlasting profit, and not for a polished phrase.
1380-1471.   —THOMAS A KEMPIS.

143 THE general diffusion of the Bible is the most effectual way to civilize and humanize mankind, to purify

and exalt the general system of public morals; to give efficacy to the just precepts of international and municipal law; to enforce the observance of prudence, temperance, justice, and fortitude; to improve all the relations of social and domestic life.

1763-1847. —JAMES KENT, Chancellor of N. Y.

144 THE Bible of the Christian is, without exception, the most remarkable work now in existence. In the libraries of the learned are frequently seen books of an extraordinary antiquity, and curious and interesting from the nature of their contents; but none approach the Bible, taken in its complete sense, in point of age, while certainly no production whatever has any pretensions to rival it in dignity of composition or the important nature of the subjects treated of in its pages. —JOHN KITTO.

1804-1854.

145 IN regard to the great Book I have only to say, it is the best book God has given to man. All the good from the Savior of the world is communicated in this Book.

    1809–1865. —ABBRAHAM LINCOLN, 16th President U. S. (to the colored men of Baltimore, who presented him with a Bible, September 14, 1864).

146 THE Bible is a book in comparison with which all others in my eyes are of minor importance, and which in all my perplexities and distresses has never failed to give me light and strength.

    — ROBERT E. LEE.
    1807–1870.

147 THE Bible is indeed the most interesting book in the world—to the poet, to the historian, to the philosopher, to the student of human nature, to the lover of the picturesque and of the marvelous, to the archæologist, to the man of letters, to the man of affairs. To each of these it

has much to say that he will find nowhere else.
  —HENRY PARRY LIDDON.
Sermon: "Supreme Value of the Scriptures," preached in St. Paul's.
1829–1890.

148 THE best literature of thirty centuries is to be found in the Bible. Warriors have fought for it; martyrs have died for it. The sacred books of the Christian, Mohammedan, and the works of the philosophers have stolen its brightest gems. It fired the eloquence of an Akiba and a Chrysostom, "upon whose lips the bees settled and left their honey there." It suggested the divine poems of Halevi, Racine, and Milton. It awoke the intrepid genius of Maimonides, Spinoza, and Mendelssohn. It inspired the pictures of Raphael, the sculptures of Angelo, the music of Mendelssohn, Meyerbeer, Handel. This Book has destroyed tyranny.
  —RABBI J. LEONARD LEVY.

149 I AM heartily glad to witness your veneration for a Book which, to say nothing of its holiness or authority, contains more specimens of genius and taste than any other volume in existence.
—WALTER SAVAGE LANDOR.
1775–1864.

150 THE Bible is the Book of life, written for the instruction and edification of all ages and nations. No man who has felt its divine beauty and power would exchange this one volume for all the literature of the world. —JOHANN PETER LANGE.
1802–1884.

151 IN morality there are books enough written, both by ancient and modern philosophers; but the morality of the Gospel doth so exceed them all, that to give a man a full knowledge of true morality I shall send him to no other book than the New Testament.
1632–1704. —JOHN LOCKE.

152 MAN can weary himself in any secular affair, but diligently to search the Scripture is to him tedious and burdensome. Few covet to be mighty in the Scriptures, though convinced their great concern is enveloped in them. —*Ibid.*

153 I CAN not attempt to describe this moral power of Holy Scripture in language. I dare not hope to add anything to the image of the text (Hebrews iv, 12, 13). The joints and the marrow of the human soul and spirit—the most complex interdependencies of passion and thought and purpose and action, and the vital center and home of the moral life—both these the Word of God probes and severs and lays bare. It is just this dissecting power, this keen penetration of the Scriptural record, which is its most wonderful moral feature. I have read in other books many wise and beautiful reflections on the relations of God and man, on life and death, on time and eternity; many lofty precepts and salutary rules for

the guidance of human conduct—much of all kinds which instructs, improves, elevates. I have read such with deep thankfulness; and I believe that all light, whatever it may be, comes from the great Father of lights. But in no other book, unless its inspiration has been derived from this Book, do I find the same delicate discrimination between the real and the seeming in things moral, the same faculty of piercing through the crust of outward conduct, and revealing the hidden springs of action, of stripping off all conventional disguises, of separating mixed motives, with their contradictory elements of good and evil. This analyzing, dissecting moral power is the logical attribute of the Written Word.

—Joseph Barber Lightfoot,
Bishop of Durham, in Cambridge Sermons.
1828-1889.

154 KINGDOMS may be moved, thrones pass away, generations go down to the valley of death, customs change, languages alter, but so long as the

earth endureth, the morality, doctrines, and precepts of the Bible shall continue among men. In vain is the cry against it, bootless the toil to make it obsolete, rash and foolish the attempt to turn it into ridicule; it is surrounded by a wall of fire, watched over by that eye which flashes destruction on its foes.

—William Leask,
"Beauties of the Bible," p. 303. Partridge & Co., London, 2d Ed.

155 BUT the child is not allowed to reject its primer because the conjunction of letters into words, and words into sentences, is a mystery; and we are not in the habit of tossing away a rose in disdain because we are ignorant concerning the mysteries of its life, its velvet texture, its colors, and its delicious fragrance; on the contrary, these all give it a sort of sacred attraction, as if it must have bloomed originally in the garden of the Lord. So the veiled mysteries of the Bible are interwoven with its tex-

ture, and impart to it a sacred beauty, of which without them it would have been destitute. —*Ibid.*, p. 17.

156 THE astonishing variety of subjects in the Bible may be thus condensed; History, like a picture, reproducing an extensive landscape; biography, immortalizing certain minds and retaining their duplicates upon the earth for the imitation or warning of subsequent generations; prophecy, anticipating the world's future; doctrines, which are clustered in the moral firmament, deep as the nature of Deity and resplendent with the luster of his brightness; precepts, which find their way direct to the heart of man; denunciations, which impress the soul with awful feelings; appeals, which demonstrate the Divine solicitude; promises, which pour the warm love of a Father's heart upon burdened souls; epistles, in which the thoughts of one man are familiarly given to another: and poetry, in which the hallelujahs of heaven are brought down to

earth, and the grand future of the Church and the world is sung in strains of rapture and bursts of magnificent imagery, such as never yet issued from uninspired pen.
—*Ibid., p. 7.*

157 THERE are no songs comparable to the songs of Zion, no orations equal to those of the prophets, and no politics like those which the Scriptures teach. —JOHN MILTON.
1608–1675.

158 IT is not hard for any man who hath a Bible in his hand to borrow good words and holy sayings in abundance.
—*Ibid.*

159 WHOEVER would acquire a knowledge of pure English must study King James's version of the Scriptures.
—THOMAS BABINGTON:
1800–1859.   (LORD MACAULAY.)

160 AT the time when the odious style which deforms the writings of Hall and of Lord Bacon was almost universal, had appeared that stupendous work, the English Bible, a Book which, if everything else in our language should perish, would alone suffice to show the whole extent of its beauty and power. —*Ibid.*

161 IT is certain, certain on the confession of its enemies, that a pure and high morality is to be gathered only from the pages of the Bible.
—HENRY MELVILLE,
Chaplain-in-ordinary to Queen Victoria.

162 WE are persuaded that there is no book by the perusal of which the mind is so much strengthened and so much enlarged as it is by the perusal of the Bible. —*Ibid.*

163 THE Bible furnishes the only fitting vehicle to express the thoughts that overwhelm us when contemplating the stellar universe.
1809-1862. —O. M. MITCHELL.

164 THE Bible makes everything speak for God. God, in these last days, has made everything speak for the Bible. Even the stone has cried out of the wall, and the beam out of the timber has answered it, "that prophecy came not in old time by the will of man, but holy men of God spake as they were moved by the Holy Ghost."
—Herbert W. Morris,
"Testimony of the Ages," p. 5.

165 WHEN you write to me, tell me the meanings of Scripture; one gem from that ocean is worth all the pebbles of earthly streams.
—Robert Murray McCheyne.
1813–1843.

166 I HAVE always found in my scientific studies that, when I could get the Bible to say anything upon the subject, it afforded me a firm platform to stand upon, and a round in the ladder by which I could safely ascend.
—Lieut. Matthew Fontaine Maury.
1806–1873.

167 THE Bible is the Word of God—with all the peculiarities of man and all the authority of God.
—Professor Murphy.

168 THE vigor of our spiritual life will be in exact proportion to the place held by the Word in our life and thoughts. I can solemnly state this from the experience of fifty-four years. The first three years after conversion I neglected, comparatively, the Word of God. Since the time I began to search it diligently the blessing has been *wonderful*. I have read since then the Bible through *one hundred times*, and each time with increasing delight. When I begin it afresh, it always seems like a new book to me. Since July, 1820, I can not tell you how great has been the blessing from *consecutive*, diligent, daily study. I look upon it as a lost day when I have not had a good time over the Word of God.
1805— —George Muller.

169 PRECISELY so has it been with these latent scientific prophecies or anticipations of the Word of God, of which we have been speaking, which seem to have been so deeply imbedded in the sacred text that the world has not seen them hitherto, nor, indeed, could see them now, were it not that our advancing science is revealing them. The geologic prophecies, though they might have been read, could not be understood till the fullness of the time had come. And it is only as the fullness of the time comes, in the brighter light of increasing scientific knowledge, that these grand old oracles of the Bible, so apparently simple, but so marvelously pregnant with meaning, stand forth at once cleared of all erroneous human glosses, and vindicated as the inspired testimonies of Jehovah.

1802-1856. —Hugh Miller.

170 INDEED, it is only in the Bible that we find a large, free, and unprejudiced history, for the reason that it

is taught incidentally. When we read Hume, we read Toryism; or Macaulay, Whiggism; and thus nearly all history is shot through with human prejudice, and wears the limitations of a single mind. But the Bible simply reflects the ages; they shine through its pages by their own light. And, above all, it gives us the secret of history; it tells us why and for what end the nations have existed, and shows us whither they are tending. And this is what a true student of history desires to learn—not how the forces were marshaled at Waterloo, but by what force and toward what goal humanity is moving.
—THEODORE T. MUNGER,
1830—   In the Christian Union.

171 AND will this old Bible of King James's version continue to be held in highest reverence? Speaking from a literary point of view, which is our standpoint to-day, there can be no doubt that it will; nor is there good reason to believe that, on literary

lines, any other will ever supplant it. There may be versions that will be truer to the Greek; there may be versions that will be far truer to the Hebrew; there may be versions that will mend its science, that will mend its archæology, and will mend its history; but never one, I think, which, as a whole, will greatly mend that orderly and musical and forceful flow of language springing from early English sources, chastened by Elizabethan culture and flowing out, freighted with Christian doctrine, over all lands where Saxon speech is uttered. Nor in saying this do I yield a jot to any one in respect for that modern scholarship which has shown bad renderings from the Greek, and possibly far worse ones from the Hebrew. No one, it is reasonably to be presumed, can safely interpret doctrines of the Bible without the aid of this scholarship and of the "higher criticism;" and no one will be henceforth fully trusted in such interpretation who is ignorant of, or who scorns, the recent revisions.

And yet the old book, by reason of its strong, sweet, literary quality, will keep its hold on most hearts and minds. —DONALD G. MITCHELL,
(Ik Marvel,) "In English Lands, Letters and Kings."
1822—

172 I FIND more sure marks of authenticity in the Bible than in any profane history whatever.
1642–1727.   — ISAAC NEWTON.

173 WE account the Scriptures of God to be the most sublime philosophy.   —*Ibid.*

174 THE Bible begins gloriously with paradise, the symbol of youth, and ends with the everlasting kingdom, with the holy city. The history of every man should be a Bible.
—NOVALIS.
Literary cognomen of Frederick von Hardenberg.
1772–1801.

175 LIKE the needle to the north pole, the Bible points to heaven.
—R. B. Nichol.

176 MEN can not be well educated without the Bible. It ought, therefore, to hold the chief place in every situation of learning throughout Christendom; and I do not know of a higher service that could be rendered to this Republic than the bringing about of this desired result.
1773–1866. —Eliphlalet Nott.

177 ALL systems of morality are fine. The gospel alone has exhibited a complete assemblage of the principles of morality divested of all absurdity. —Napoleon I.
1768–1821.

178 BOOK unique! Who but God could produce that idea of perfection, equally exclusive and original? —*Ibid.*

179 THE Bible contains a complete series of facts, and of historical men, to explain time and eternity, such as no other religion has to offer. Everything in it is grand and worthy of God. Even the impious themselves have never dared to deny the sublimity of the Gospel, which inspires them with a sort of compulsory veneration. —*Ibid.*

180 THE Gospel is not merely a book, it is a living power—a Book surpassing all others. I never omit to read it, and every day with the same pleasure. Nowhere is to be found such a series of beautiful ideas and admirable moral maxims, which pass before us like the battalions of a celestial army. The soul can never go astray with this Book for its guide. —*Ibid.*

181 BEFORE the literature of Greece had been thought of, song and story and the noblest inspirations of philosophy and poetry had come into

being upon the little crests of Zion and Moriah; the Temple had been there which has never faded, though destroyed, burned, broken down a dozen times, swept far from sight and knowledge, from the memory and imagination of men; and the records of humanity had begun to be put forth in full splendor of character and impulse and feeling, in chronicles which are as fresh and living now as when they were the transcripts of the life of three thousand years ago. We go no farther than the heroic age of Hebrew genius when we name this date; beyond, in the midst of the ages, before even ancient Egypt had begun to engrave her rigid annals upon stone, the record goes back, not in hieroglyphics, but in histories of living men. A learned sect studies and scrutinizes with painful confusion of images what a great Rameses may or may not have done; but the child of to-day wants no better entertainment than that story of Joseph and his brethren, which is told in every language, and never fails to touch the simple heart. Before Homer had begun his primitive minstrel strain to celebrate the fights and wiles of the chiefs and kings, Isaiah had risen to the highest heights of poetry, had opened the dim gates of Hades, and had revealed, on the other hand, a dazzling glimpse of a heaven in which one God sat upon a throne of light and judged and tried the spirits of men. There is no such record in all the histories. The Psalms which began with David breathe forth the deepest emotions of our race to-day. The wisdom which, throughout all the tenacious East, bears the name of Solomon, has never been outpassed by any successor. And when we descend the course of the ages and come to a still more glorious and wonderful history, it is Jerusalem still which is the scene both of tragedy and triumph, of the greatest and most wonderful life which was ever lived among men.

—Margaret Wilson Oliphant,
1828—   In "Jerusalem."

182 THE pure and noble, the graceful and dignified simplicity of language is nowhere in such perfection as in the Scriptures.

 1688-1744. —ALEXANDER POPE,

183 IN a word, destroy this volume, and you take from us at once everything which prevents existence becoming of all curses the greatest; you blot out the sun, dry up the ocean, and take away the atmosphere of the moral world; and degrade man to a situation from which he may look up with envy to that of the brutes that perish. —EDWARD PAYSON,

 1783-1827.

184 SCARCELY can we fix our eyes upon a single passage in this wonderful Book which has not afforded comfort and instruction to thousands, and been met with tears of penitential sorrow or grateful joy drawn from eyes that will weep no more.

 —*Ibid.*

185 THE answer to the Shaster is India; the answer to Confucianism is China; the answer to the Koran is Turkey; the answer to the Bible is the Christian civilization of Protestant Europe and America.
1811-1884. —WENDELL PHILLIPS.

186 MOST wondrous book! bright candle of the Lord!
Star of eternity! the only star
By which the bark of man could navigate
The sea of life, and gain the coast of bliss
Securely. —ROBERT POLLOK.
1798-1827.

187 THIS lamp from off the everlasting throne
Mercy took down, and in the night of time,
Stood casting on the dark her gracious bow,
And evermore beseeching men, with tears
And earnest sighs, to hear, believe, and live. —*Ibid.*

188 THIS Book, this holy Book, on every line
Marked with the seal of high divinity—
On every leaf bedewed with drops of love
Divine, and with the eternal heraldry
And signature of God Almighty stamped
From first to last. —*Ibid.*

189 THE Bible goes equally to the cottage of the plain man and the palace of the king. It is woven into literature, and it colors the talk of the street. The bark of the merchant can not sail to sea without it. No ship of war goes to the conflict but the Bible is there. It enters men's closets, mingling in all grief and cheerfulness of life.
1810-1871. —THEODORE PARKER.

190 SOME thousand famous writers come up in this century, to be forgotten in the next. But the silver cord of the Bible is not loosed, nor

its golden bowl broken, though time chronicles his tens of centuries passed by. —*Ibid.*

191 YOU can trace the path of the Bible across the world from the day of Pentecost to this day. As a river springs up in the heart of a sandy continent, having its father in the skies; as the stream rolls on, making, in that arid waste, a belt of verdure wherever it turns its way, creating palm-groves and fertile plains, where the smoke of the cottage curls up at eventide, and marble cities send the gleam of their splendor far into the sky: such has been the course of the Bible on earth. There is not a boy on all the hills of New England; not a girl born in the filthiest cellar which disgraces a captal in Europe, and cries to God against the barbarism of modern civilization; not a boy nor a girl all Christendom through, but their lot is made better by that great Book. —*Ibid.*

192 I HAVE always felt atttached to this Divine production, even when I have not believed myself one of its avowed followers. With the love of God and mankind, it inspired me also with a veneration for justice and an abhorrence of wickedness, along with a desire of pardoning the wicked.
 1789-1854. —SILVIO PELLICO.

193 I LOVE the Bible. I read it every day; and the more I read it, the more I love it. There are some people who do not love the Bible. I do not understand them. I do not understand such people, but I love it; I love its simplicity, and I love its very repetitions and reiterations of truth. As I said, I read it daily, and the more I read it, the more I love it.
 —THE EMPEROR DOM PEDRO II.,
In conversation with Rev. J. C. Fletcher, reported in the N. Y. Evangelist.
 1825-1891.

194 THERE is no one book extant in any one language, or in any country, which can in any degree be com-

pared with the Bible for antiquity, for authority, for the importance, the dignity, the variety, and the curiosity of the matter it contains.

—BEILBY PORTEUS,
1731–1808.   Bishop of London.

195 THE Scriptures, having been written at different periods and in divers languages, requiring for their interpretation the aid of knowledge that is always increasing, not only may, but must give forth fresh light with each new century.

1811–1892.   —NOAH PORTER,
From Sermon on "Religious Progress," in the Independent.

196 AFTER reading the doctrines of Plato, Socrates, or Aristotle, we feel that the specific difference between their words and Christ's is the difference between an inquiry and a revelation.   —JOSEPH PARKER.

197 I AM impressed by the abundant evidence that your style has been unconsciously formed by your famil-

iarity with our English Bible, which has a unique worth in shaping a diction equally pure, dignified, easy, graceful, and euphonious. Did I know nothing about you personally, I should infer from your books that you have that thorough acquaintance with the *ipsissima verba* of our Bible, which was much more common in your and in my earlier days than I fear it is among even the sincere Christians of a younger generation. I am accustomed to say to young men who are ambitious to write well: "Study the English Bible. It will be worth more to you than all oral or written rules, and than all other examples of English composition."
—Andrew Preston Peabody,
To an American Author.
1811–1893.

198 THE most highly-valued treasure of every family library, and that most frequently and lovingly made use of, should be the Holy Scriptures.
—Plenary Council,
At Baltimore, 1884.

199 SOME words excell in vertue, and discover
A rare condition, thrice repeated over.
Our Saviour thrice was tempted; thrice represt
The assaulting tempter with thrice *Scriptus est.*
If thou wouldst keep thy soule secure from harme,
Thou know'st the words: It is a potent charme.

. . . .

God's Sacred Word is like the Lampe of Day
Which softens wax, but makes obdure the clay;
It either melts the heart, or more obdures;
It never falls in vain: It wounds or cures.
    1592–1644. —FRANCIS QUARLES,
      In " Divine Fancies," 1641 A. D.

200 I MUST confess the majesty of the Scriptures astonishes me.
        —JEAN JACQUES ROUSSEAU.
1712–1778.

201 HOW petty are the books of the philosphers, with all their pomp, compared to the Gospels! —*Ibid.*

202 A BAD heart is the great objection against the Holy Book.
 1648–1680. —JOHN WILMOT,
    Earl of Rochester.

203 CHRISTIANITY is the only true and perfect religion, and in proportion as mankind adopt its principles and obey its precepts, they will be wise and happy. And a better knowledge of this religion is to be acquired by reading the Bible than in any other way.
 1741–1813. —BENJAMIN RUSH.

204 I WILL answer for it, the longer you read the Bible, the more you will like it. It will grow sweeter and sweeter; and the more you get into the spirit of it, the more you will get into the Spirit of Christ.
 1714–1795. —WILLIAM ROMAINE.

205 THIS Book has held spell-bound the hearts of nations in a way in which no single Book has ever held men before. States have been founded on its principles. Men hold the Bible in their hands when they prepare to give solemn evidence affecting life.
—FREDERICK W. ROBERTSON.
1816–1853.

206 IF all the books were placed in one library, and this single One set on a table in the middle of it, and a stranger were told that this Book, affirmed to be for the most part the work of a number of unlearned and obscure men, belonging to a despised nation called the Jews, and had drawn upon itself for its exposure, confutation, and destruction, this multitude of volumes,—I imagine he would be inclined to say: "Then, I presume, this little Book was annihilated long ago; though how it could be needful to write a thousandth part so much for any such purpose I can not comprehend; for if the book be what these

authors say, surely it should not be difficult to show it to be so; and if so, what wonderful madness to write all these volumes!" How surprised would he then be to learn that they were felt not to be *enough;* that similar works were being multiplied every day, and never more actively than at the present time.

—Henry Rodgers,
"Superhuman Origin of the Bible," p. 254.

207 THE Book which has given them all their ephemeral renown, seems alone untouched by time. It is like some old oak which has seen the harvest of a thousand years' springs ripen and fall beneath the sickle. —*Ibid., p.* 279.

208 THE Bible is not such a Book as man would have made if he could, or could have made if he would have done so. —*Ibid., p.* 5.

209 TO my early knowledge of the Bible I owe the best part of my taste in literature and the most pre-

cious and, on the whole, the one essential part of my education.
1819— —JOHN RUSKIN.

210 I HAVE been blamed for the familiar application of its sacred words. I am grieved to have given pain by so doing; but my excuse must be my wish that those words were made the ground of every argument and the test of every action. We have them not often enough upon our lips, nor deeply enough in our memories, nor loyally enough in our lives. The snow, the vapor, and the stormy wind fulfill His word. Are our acts and thoughts lighter and wilder than these, that we should forget it?
—*Ibid.*

211 "AFTER our chapters (from two to three a day, according to their length), the first thing after breakfast (and no interruptions from servants allowed, none from visitors, who either joined in the reading or had to stay up-stairs, and none from any visiting or excursions, except real trav-

eling), I had to learn a few verses by heart, or repeat, to make sure I had not lost something of what was already known; and, with the chapters thus gradually possessed from the first to the last, I had to learn the whole body of the fine old Scotch paraphrases, which are good, melodious, and forceful verses, and to which, together with the Bible itself, I owe the first cultivation of my ear in sound." Mr. Ruskin prints his mother's list of the chapters, "with which, thus learned, she established my soul in life." It is as follows: Exodus, chapters xv, xvi; 2 Samuel i, from the seventeenth verse to the end; 1 Kings viii; Psalms xxii, xxxiii, xc, xci, ciii, cxii, cxix, cxxxix; Proverbs chapters ii, iii, viii, xii; Isaiah lviii; Matthew, chapters v, vi, vii; Acts xxvi; 1 Corinthians, chapters xiii, xv; James iv; Revelation, chapters v, vi. And truly Mr. Ruskin says: "Though I have picked up the elements of a little further knowledge—in mathematics, meteorology, and the like, in after life—and owe not a little to the teach-

ing of many people, this material installation of my mind in that property of chapters I count very confidently the most precious, and, on the whole, the one essential part of my education."   JOHN RUSKIN,
In "Autobiography."

212 WALTER SCOTT and Alexander Pope were the reading of my own early election; but my mother forced me to read the Bible from Genesis to Apocalypse, and to that discipline, patient, accurate, resolute, I owe not only a knowledge of the Bible, but the best part of my taste in literature. . . . Knowing by heart the hundred and nineteenth Psalm, the Sermon on the Mount, and other places of Holy Scripture, it was not possible for me to write entirely superficial English. —*Ibid.*, in "Fors Clavigeræ."

213 I SEE in your columns, as in other journals, more and more buzzing and fussing about what M. Rénan has found the Bible to be, or Mr. Huxley not to be, or the bishops that it might be, or the school board that it must n't be, etc. Let me tell your readers who care to know, in the fewest possible words what it *is*. It is the grandest group of writings existent in the rational world, put into the grandest language of the rational world, in the first strength of the Christian faith, by an entirely wise and kind saint, St. Jerome; translated afterward with beauty and felicity into every language of the Christian world; and the guide, since so translated, of all the arts and acts of that world which have been noble, fortunate, and happy. And by consultation of it honestly, on any serious business, you may always learn—a long while before your Parliament finds out—what you should do in such business, and be directed perhaps besides to work more serious than you had thought of.

—*Ibid.*, in the Pall Mall Gazette.

214 FATHER of Mercies, in thy Word
  What endless glory shines!
Forever be thy name adored
  For these celestial lines.
  1717-1778.   —ANNE STEELE.

215 I KNOW that what I read and possess in the Word will remain when the world passes away, and that its slightest sentence will prove a better dying pillow than all else that man could conceive or possess.
  1800-1862.   —RUDOLF STIER.

216 ONE Book alone has outlasted many generations, in all nations equally, and that is the Bible; and this is because of its exceeding breadth—because it embraces every variety and element of thought, and every phase of society; above all, because it embodies in every part the moral commandment of God, which endures forever in heaven, and which applies not to one condition of life only, but to all.
  —ARTHUR PENRHYN STANLEY,
  1815-1881.   Dean of Westminster.

217 BUT we ought not to tremble too much for the ark of God; it is God's ark, and he will take charge of it. This is only an episode in the history of the Bible; the providence of God is watching over it; and we may be very sure that when it is over, the Bible, being better understood, will be seen more clearly than ever to be suited to the deepest wants of man, and fitted to be the torch which guides him along the pathway of progress. —JAMES STALKER,
75th Anniversary Amer. Bible Society,

218 THE whole hope of human progress is suspended on the ever-growing influence of the Bible.
 1801–1872. —WILLIAM H. SEWARD.

219 NOBODY ever outgrows Scripture. The Book widens and deepens with our years.
 —CHARLES H. SPURGEON.
 1834–1892.

220 EVEN the style of the Scriptures is more than human. —STEELE.

221 THE popular reverence for the Bible is also strong, and it extends to every copy of the printed Book, and includes even those who reject the supernatural authority of Scripture. At least so far as the exhibition of outward and formal respect is concerned, they are all of one mind. The various Bible societies are careful to put copies of the Scriptures in the reading-rooms and bedrooms of hotels and upon all ships and steamers. It can not be said that those volumes give evidences of having been extensively read, but they are never defaced. The most flippant treat the Holy Bible with instinctive and distinctive respect.
—NEW YORK SUN.

222 UNLIKE other books, the Bible has neither preface nor introduction. Nor has it definitions, postulates, axioms, or elementary theorems on which to build its science of the-

ology or to prepare its students for its higher revelations or developments. Its first words bring us face to face with eternity and divinity.
MATTHEW SIMPSON,

Lecture: Majesty and Holiness of Bible. God's Word, Man's Light and Guide. Lectures before N. Y. S. S. Association, American Tract Society.
1811–1884.

223 I HAVE surveyed most of the learning that is among the children of men, yet at this moment I recall nothing in them on which to rest my soul save one from the sacred Scriptures which rises much on my mind: "The grace of God which bringeth salvation hath appeared unto all men."
—JOHN SELDEN,
1584–1658.   To Archbishop Usher.

224 VIEWED merely as a literary production, the Bible is a marvelous Book, and without a rival. All the libraries of theology, philosophy, history, antiquities, poetry, law, and

policy would not furnish material enough for so rich a treasure of the choicest gems of human genius, wisdom, and experience.

 1819-1893.   —Philip Schaff.

225 THE translators of the Bible were makers of our English style much fitter for that work than any we see in our present writings. The which is owing to the simplicity that runs through the whole.

  —Jonathan Swift,
  Dean of St. Patrick's, Dublin.
 1667-1745.

226 LET us cling with a holy zeal to the Bible, and the Bible only, as the religion of Protestants. Let us proclaim, with Milton, that neither traditions, nor councils, nor canons of visible Church, much less edicts of any civil magistrate or civil session, but the Scriptures only, can be the final judge or rule. —Joseph Story,
  Justice Supreme Court, U. S.
 1779-1845.

227 IN the whole compass of poetry there is nothing more poetical, more musical, more thrilling, and, in some passages, more full of lofty inspiration than the Psalms of David.
—HENRY STEPHANUS.

228 HE who has once gained this broader view of the Bible as the development of a course of history itself, guided and inspired by Jehovah, will not be disconcerted by the confused noises of the critic. His faith in the Word of God lies deeper than any difficulties or flaws upon the surface of the Bible. He will not be disturbed by seeing any theory of its mechanical formation or schoolbook infallibility broken to fragments under the repeated blows of modern investigation. The water of life will flow from the rock which the scholar strikes with his rod.
—NEWMAN SMYTH,
"Old Faiths in New Lights," p. 59.
1843—

229 THE Bible has been the potent interpreter of the spiritual instincts of a considerable portion of our race, giving form and voice and force to their thoughts of God, of duty, of judgment and the life to come throughout the length and breadth of the Christian world.
—VANCE SMITH,
"The Bible and its Theology," p. 300.

230 WHEN you can prove to me that man has built the mountains of brick-work and has covered the earth with a mud which he has manufactured for soil, then you may prove to me that the Bible, with its oneness and variety, its production extending over fifteen hundred years, with its last verse answering to its first across the dreary drift of ages, has come to us from man.
1821—   —RICHARD S. STORRS.

231 ALMOST every feeling finds a voice in the Psalms. But here are not their only expressions. The prophecies contain them. They break upon us through scores of narratives and in hundreds of incidents. And there is not a note of human emotion, from the plaint of despondency or the wail of despair up to the noblest Christian war-hymn—yea, up to the very *Te Deum* of saints celebrating the final attainment of heaven—that is not somewhere sounded in the Bible. —*Ibid.*

Sermon: Jubilee American Bible Society, 1866.

232 THE most learned, acute, and diligent student can not in the longest life obtain an entire knowledge of this one volume. The more deeply he works the mine, the richer and more abundant he finds the ore; new light continually beams from this source of heavenly knowledge, to direct the conduct and illustrate the works of God and the ways of men; and he will at last leave the world confessing that the more he studied the Scriptures the fuller conviction he had of his own ignorance and of their inestimable value. — WALTER SCOTT. 1771–1832.

233 WITHIN this awful volume lies
　　The mystery of mysteries;
Happiest they of human race
To whom their God has given grace
To read, to fear, to hope, to pray,
To lift the latch, to force the way;
But better had they ne'er been born,
That read to doubt, or read to scorn.
　　　　　　　　—*Ibid.*
　　　　　"The Monastery."

234 MANY a fathom dark and deep
　　I have laid the Book to sleep,
Ethereal fires around it glowing—
Ethereal music ever flowing—
The sacred pledge of Heaven.
　　All things revere,
　　Each in his sphere,
Save man for whom 'twas given;
Lend thy hand and thou shalt spy
Things ne'er seen by mortal eye.
　　　　　　　　—*Ibid.*
　　　　　"The Monastery."

"THERE IS BUT ONE BOOK."

[From the last words of Sir Walter Scott.]

235 FETCH me the Buke, dear Lockhart,
    An' gie me ane sweet ward.
What buke? There is nae ither,—
    The Life o' th' Incarnate Lord;
I feel the shadows creepin';
    My licht's nae burnin' lang,
Sae read frae the blessit Gospels
    A bit, chiel, ere I gang;
Fin' whaur He holpit the needy,
    His pity wi' His micht!
O, my soul's fair hungry, Lockhart,
    For the Livin' Bread, the nicht.

I think o' the dear disciples
    Sae tassit on the sea,
An' the wards He spak' tae Simon,—
    I ken they'd comfort me;
Tell o' the chitterin' sparrows,—
    "Nae wan o' them can' fa';"
Tell hoo He callit the bairnies,—
    The dearest thocht o' a',
Read owre hoo the ravin' tempest
    Seekit silence i' the deep;
Sae the surges i' my bosom
    Are croonin' a' tae sleep;

Ye maun catch the roll o' Jordan
   I' His wards tae the Pharisee,
But ye'll hear Him prayin' dearie,
   I' the sough o' Galilee;
Dinnah fash 'bout Judas kisses;
   Nae greet i' the garden dim,
But joy hoo the dyin' beggar
   Foun' paradise wi Him;
Nae hent o' Thamas dootin',
   Nae ward hoo Peter fell;
It grie's me, sair,—their weakness
   Wha ken't oor Lord sae weel;

Read o' the walk tae Emmaus
   That long an' tearfu' day,
An lat oor hearts burn, Lockhart,
   As we gang the countrie way;
Pluck me ane lily, Lockhart,
   A' siller-dew't an' sweet;
I speer the rose o' Sharon,
   An' smell the growin' wheat;
Lat's join the throngin', dearie,
   An' wait i' the wee bit ships
For the ward, like beads o' honey,
   That fa' frae His haly lips.

Hoo sad the Gospels, Lockhart,
   Wi' his wand'rin' hameless life!

But there 's ane grief fetches comfort,
  Ane rest that comes o' strife:
Noo tak' me, kin', gude Lockhart,—
  Aye tenner-true tae me!—
Oot wi' the dear disciples,
  "As far 's tae Bethany;"
I sair need rest, belov'd,
  An' the licht 's a-wearin' dim;
But heaven's nae far fra Bethany,
  An' sune I'll be wi' Him.
      —AGNES E. MITCHELL.

236 GOOD heaven, were the truths of the Book prevalent in the hearts of men, should we be disturbed and frightened as we are day by day by those gigantic frauds that are bursting out in every community, and which lead us to believe that all honesty in trade, all honesty in public life, all honesty in private life, have left the world forever? Is it unsuited to the times in which we live, when, if its holy precepts and its Divine commands had been listened to, we should not have these gigantic evils?
  —THE 7TH EARL OF SHAFTESBURY,
      Life of. Vol. I, p. 7.

237 AH! but now they come and tell us that the Bible is effete; that it is worn out; that it can do nothing, and that we must now have some new influence, some new principle, by which to regulate and guide man. Effete! Indeed, I should like to know whether it is effete at this moment in India. Is it effete in the effect, lately begun, to be produced in China? Is it effete in the islands of the Pacific Ocean? Is it effete in Madagascar? Is it effete in Italy? You see what a country Italy has now become; you see how the Italians are now grasping at the Word of God, and although they have not thrown off the trammels of the Church of Rome, they have imbibed the first principles, whereby their conduct in public and private life should be guided. The Bible lies at the root of their freedom, and they know it well enough to make it the basis of their hopes and fears. That is the Book that will guide them. —*Ibid.*, Vol. I, p. 7.

238 DO the Neologists themselves think it effete? If so, why do they pass their nights, why do they sweat and toil over the midnight lamp, for the sole purpose of destroying a Book that is so effete that, if left to itself, would soon die or become an object of general contempt? They do not think it effete. They know its power upon the heart and the conscience. They know that, if left to itself, that good old Book must work its own way, and what they deny with their lips they confess with their fears. Effete? It is effete as Abraham was effete, when he became the father of many nations, when they sprang of one, and him as good as dead, as many as the stars for multitude and the sands upon the seashore innumerable. It is effete as eternity past, present, and future is effete. It is effete, and in no other sense, as God himself is effete—the same yesterday, to-day, and forever.

—*Ibid.*, Vol. I, p. 8.

239 SAVE for my daily range
  Among the pleasant fields of Holy Writ,
I might despair.
  —ALFRED, LORD TENNYSON.
  1809–1892.

240 WITH the history of Moses, no book in the world, in point of antiquity, can contend.
  1630-1694. —JOHN TILLOTSON,
    Archbishop of Canterbury.

241 HOLY Scripture becomes resplendent, or, as one might say, incandescent throughout.
  1787–1865.   —ISAAC TAYLOR.

242 THE integrity of the records of the Christian faith is substantiated by evidence in a tenfold proportion more various, copious, and conclusive than that which can be adduced in support of any other ancient writings.
  —*Ibid.*

243   AS the profoundest philosophy of ancient Rome and Greece lighted her taper at Israel's altar, so the sweetest strains of the pagan muse were swept from harps attuned on Zion's Hill.
—EDWARD THOMSON.
1810–1870.

244   THE Bible is a thing of light, and illumines whatsoever it shines upon; a thing of beauty, and adorns whatsoever it touches; a thing of life, and quickens whatsoever it comes in contact with.
—W. TRAIL,
"Literary Characteristics and Achievements of the Bible." (Clergyman.)

245   THE man of one book is always formidable; but when that Book is the Bible, he is irresistible.
1829–1896. —WILLIAM M. TAYLOR.

246   THE Book is literature, and not mere theology. Its moral precepts and ever-to-be-remembered stories of fidelity and self-sacrifice

never lose their wonted charm or grandeur.
—Boston Evening Transcript, Saturday, April 11, 1896.

247 THE present-day critical investigation of the Bible may in some respects modify or change the popular conception of it. Indeed, it has done so in a measure already; but in so far as we can see, it has in no degree weakened the hold of the Bible on the conscience of Christendom. Nor is there the faintest sign that modern civilization intends to part with any of the essential principles and ideals which it has learned from that venerable Book. Possibly Moses may have made mistakes; he was great enough to do so. But no mistake he ever made compares with that of those who think to elevate and ennoble the world by splitting "the ears of the groundlings" with coarse sneers at religion and the Bible.   —The New York Tribune.

248 IMMENSELY as the literature of this country has increased in this century, the Bible now occupies a larger proportionate space in that literature than ever it did. No Book raises so many inquiries or touches so many interests. The Bible sends the student to libraries and archives. To the Bible we owe much of the intense and spreading interest in languages and in the originals of customs and of peoples. It directs the traveler to buried cities, to the tombs of kings, to the records of States once great, and well-nigh forgotten. Wherever the battle of opinion is now the liveliest, wherever the race for discovery is most eager, wherever the earth at last reveals her buried history, it is to add to our knowledge of the sacred story, and to our understanding of the sacred volume.

—The London Times.

249 THE man who recreated the German language—I hardly think the expression too strong—was Martin Luther. It was his fortune and that of the world that he was so equally great in many directions— as a personal character, as a man of action, as a teacher and preacher, and finally as an author. No one before him, and no one for nearly two hundred years after him, saw that the German tongue must be sought for in the mouths of the people—that the exhausted expression of the earlier ages could not be revived, but that the newer, fuller, and richer speech, then in its childhood, must at once be acknowledged and adopted. He made it the vehicle of what was divinest in human language; and those who are not informed of his manner of translating the Bible, can not appreciate the originality of his work, or the marvelous truth of the instinct which led him to it.

With all his scholarship, Luther dropped the theological style, and sought among the people for phrases as artless and simple as those of the Hebrew writers. He frequented the market-place, the merry-making, the house of birth, marriage, or death among the common people, in order to catch the fullest expression of their feelings in the simplest words. He enlisted his friends in the same service, begging them to note down for him any peculiar, sententious phrase; "for," said he, "I can not use the words heard in castles and at courts." Not a sentence of the Bible was translated until he had sought for the briefest, clearest, and strongest German equivalent to it. He writes, in 1530: "I have exerted myself, in translating, to give pure and clear German. And it has verily happened that we have sought and questioned a fortnight, three, four weeks, for a single word, and yet it was not always found. In Job we so labored—Philip Melanchthon, Aurogallus, and I—that in four days we sometimes barely finished three lines. . . . It is well enough to plow when the field is cleared; but to root out stock and stone, and prepare the ground, is what no one will."

He illustrates his own plan of translation by an example which is so interesting that I must quote it: "We must not ask the men of letters in the Latin language how we should speak German, as the asses do; but we must ask the mother in the house, the children in the lanes, the common man in the market-place, and read in their mouths how they speak, and translate according thereto; then they understand, for they see we are speaking German to them. As when Christ says: *Ex abundantia cordis os loquitur*. Now if I were to follow the asses, they would dissect for me the letters and thus translate: 'Out of the superabundance of the heart speaks the mouth.' Now tell me is that spoken German? No German would say that, unless he meant that he had too much of a heart, although even that is not correct; for superabundance of heart is not German, any more than superabudance of house, superabundance of cooking-stove, superabundance of bench; but thus speaketh the mother in the house and the common man: 'Whose heart is full, his mouth overflows.' That is Germanly spoken, such as I have endeavored to do, but alas! not always succeeded."

Luther translated the Bible eighty years before our English version was produced. I do not know whether the English translators made any use of his labors, although they inclined toward the same plan, without following it so conscientiously. In regard to the accuracy of rendering, there is less difference. But in regard to the fullness, the strength, the tenderness, the vital power of language, I think Luther's Bible decidedly superior to our own. The instinct of one great man is in such matters, if not a safer, at least a more satisfactory guide than the average judgment of forty-seven men. Luther was a poet as well as a theologian, and as a poet he was able to feel, as no theologian could, the intrinsic difference of spirit and character in the different books of the Old Testament—not only to feel, but, through the sympathetic quality of the poetic nature, to reproduce them. These

ten years, from 1522 to 1532, which he devoted to the work, were not only years of unremitting, prayerful, conscientious labor, but also of warm, bright, joyous, intellectual creation. We can only appreciate his wonderful achievement by comparing it with any German prose before his time.
1825-1878. —BAYARD TAYLOR,
Studies in German Literature.

250 AFTER all, the Bible must be its own argument and defense. The power of it can never be proved unless it is felt. The authority of it can never be supported unless it is manifest. The light of it can never be demonstrated unless it shines.
—H. J. VAN DYKE.

251 FROM the time that, at my mother's feet or on my father's knee, I first learned to lisp verses from the Sacred Writings, they have been my daily study and vigilant contemplation. —DANIEL WEBSTER.
1782-1852.

252 I HAVE read the Bible through many times; I now make a practice of going through it once a year. It is the Book of all others for lawyers as well as divines; and I pity the man who can not find in it a rich supply of thought and rules for conduct. —*Ibid.*

253 MY style in language and thought is due to my early love of the Scriptures. —*Ibid.*

254 THE biography of the seventh Earl of Shaftesbury contains a letter addressed to him by Daniel Webster, dated Washington, May 7, 1840, which begins as follows:

"DEAR LORD ASHLEY,—I owe you many thanks for a kind note which I received at the moment of my departure from London last autumn, and for the present of a copy of a very excellent edition of the Holy Bible. You could have given me nothing more acceptable, and I shall keep it near me, as a valued token of your regard. The older I grow, and the more I read the Holy Scriptures, the more reverence I have for them, and the more convinced I am that they are not only the best guide for the conduct of this life, but the foundation of all hope respecting a future state of existence." —*Ibid.*

255 I BELIEVE that the Bible is to be understood and received in the plain and obvious meaning of its passages; for I can not persuade myself that a Book intended for the instruction and conversion of the whole world should cover its true meaning in any such mystery and doubt that none but critics and philosophers can discover it. —*Ibid.*

256 IF we abide by the principles taught in the Bible, our country will go on prospering and to prosper; but if we and our posterity neglect its instructions and authority, no man can tell how sudden a catastrophe may overwhelm us, and bury all our glory in profound obscurity. —*Ibid.*

257 PHILOSOPHICAL argument, especially that drawn from the vastness of the universe in comparison with the comparative insignificance of this globe, has sometimes shaken my reason for the faith that is in me; but my heart has always assured and re-assured me that the Gospel of Jesus Christ must be a Divine reality.

—*Ibid.*

258 THE misfortunes of China seem likely to bring her to a more teachable mood. One of the symptoms of a new feeling is the acceptance by the dowager empress, on the sixtieth anniversary of her birthday, of a Bible in the Chinese language, for which she expressed her grateful thanks, at the same time promising to read it. What is more significant is, that the emperor last week sent one of the chief officers of his household to the Bible Society's depot, to purchase a copy of the Scriptures similar to the one presented to the empress. —Christian World.

259 THE Bible is a rock of diamonds, a chain of pearls, the sword of the Spirit, a chart by which the Christian sails to eternity, the map by which he daily walks, the sun-dial by which he sets his life, the balance in which he weighs his actions.
 1690   —T. WATSON.

260 THAT the truths of the Bible have the power of awakening an intense moral feeling in every human being; that they make bad men good, and send a pulse of healthful feeling through all the domestic, civil, and social relations; that they teach men to love right and hate wrong, and seek each other's welfare, as children of a common parent; that they control the baleful passions of the heart, and thus make men proficient in self-government; and, finally, that they teach man to aspire after conformity to a Being of infinite holiness, and fill him with hopes more purifying, exalted, and suited to his nature, than any other book the

world has ever known,—these are facts as incontrovertible as the laws of philosophy or the demonstrations of mathematics.

 1796-1865. —Francis Wayland.

261 WE search the world for truth, we cull
The good, the pure, the beautiful,
From graven stone and written scroll,
From the old flower-fields of the soul,
And, weary seekers for the best,
We come back laden from our quest,
To find that all the sages said
Is in the Book our mothers read.
  —John Greenleaf Whittier.
1807-1892.

262 IT is sheer waste of time to quarrel about modes of inspiration. Let the Book prove its own inspiration. When we read it, we feel its power. When we give it to others, it proves its divineness. The flowing tide is with the Bible, and, as the tide rises, the brawling streams by its shores are hushed. Send on the Book, and

see what it will do. It makes the savage a man. It strikes from the captive his chains, and makes the freeman more free. It fills civilized communities with the voices of love in its purity, and the pledges of friendship in its faithfulness. The Word that has gone forth out of God's mouth will prove the power of God; and the more we read that Word ourselves, we shall be able to say with greater confidence, "It is my Bible."
—William Wright.

263 IN Job and the Psalms we shall find more sublime ideas, more elevated language, than in any of the heathen versifiers of Greece or Rome.
    1674–1748.   Isaac Watts.

264 COMPARE the Book of Psalms with the Odes of Horace or Anacreon, with the Hymns of Callimachus, the Golden Verses of Pythagoras, the Choruses of the Greek tragedians, and you will quickly see how greatly it surpasses them all in

piety of sentiment, in sublimity of expression, in purity of morality, and in rational theology.

 1737-1816. —RICHARD WATSON,
      Bishop of Llandaff.
"An Apology for the Bible. Reply to Paine's 'Age of Reason.'"

265 THIS, for my part, I do believe, that the Scripture is clear and full of light, as to all matters of conscience, as to all rules of light, as to all necessary matters of faith, so that any well-minded man that takes up the Bible and reads, may come to understanding and satisfaction. And to this purpose then is the Divine Spirit to wait upon this instrument of God.
    —BENJAMIN WHICHCOTE.
 1610-1683.

266 STAR of eternity! The only star
  By which the bark of man could navigate
 The sea of life, and gain the coast of bliss
 Securely; only star which rose on Time,

And, on its dark and troubled billows,
    still,
As generation, difting swifly by,
Succeeded generation, threw a ray
Of Heaven's own light, and to the
    hills of God,
The eternal hills, pointed the sinner's
    eye. —ALEXANDER WALLACE.

267 DIFFUSE the knowledge of the Bible, and the hungry will be fed and the naked clothed. Diffuse the knowledge of the Bible and the stranger will be sheltered, the prisoner visited, and the sick ministered unto. Diffuse the knowledge of the Bible and temperance will rest upon a surer basis than any mere private pledge or public statute.
    1809—   —ROBERT C. WINTHROP.

268 THERE are in Shakespeare's works more than five hundred and fifty Biblical quotations, allusions, references, and sentiments. "Hamlet" alone contains about eighty, "Richard the Third" nearly fifty, "Henry

the Fifth " and Richard the Second "
about forty each. Shakespeare quotes
from fifty-four of the Biblical books,
and not one of his thirty-seven plays
is without a Scriptural reference.
Genesis furnishes the poet thirty-one
quotations or allusions, the Psalms
with fifty-nine, Proverbs with thirty-
five, Isaiah with twenty-one, Matthew
with sixty, Luke with thirty, and Ro-
mans with twenty.

 1807— Bishop Wordsworth,
   Shakespeare and the Bible.

269 TURN from the oracles of man,
still dim even in their clearest re-
ponse, to the oracles of God, which
are never dark. Bury all your books
when you feel the night of skepticism
gathering around you; bury them all,
powerful though you may have
deemed their spells to illuminate the
unfathomable; open your Bible, and
all the spiritual world will be bright
as day.

 —John Wilson (Christopher North).
  1785–1854.

270 IT is my earnest wish, gentlemen, that the words you have just heard from the pulpit may find place and realization in the hearts and thoughts of all. . . . If there is anything that, amidst the drifting stress of the world's life, can give us a holdfast, it is the one, the solitary, foundation which is laid in Jesus Christ. Do not allow yourselves to be bewildered into missing this, gentlemen, by the flux of change which, especially at the present period, traverses the world. Do not join the multitude of those who either ignore the Bible altogether as the one foundation of truth, or at least give it a spurious interpretation of their own devising. You all know that I am a member, on full and free conviction, of the "Positive Union" established by my late dear father. The basis and rock on which I, and we all, are bound to fix our foothold, is the unadulterated faith as taught us by the Bible. There are, to be sure, many who do not all take exactly the same line of interpretation; each uses his knowledge and conscience as well as he can, and thereby regulates his acts and purposes. . . . May all the Alumni of this institution find this day so blest to them that the knowledge of God and his only-begotten Son Jesus Christ, as the alone source of true salvation, may advance in them! Each indeed is free to deal with this according to the voice of his conscience; but all must build on the foundation of the Bible and the Gospel. Let but this be secured, and all will be enabled to develop a Divinely-blest ministerial work, each according to his special gift.

1859— —THE EMPEROR WILLIAM,
In an Adress at the Jubilee of the Cathedral College for Candidates for Orders.

271 RETIRE and read thy Bible, to be gay;
There truths abound of sovereign aid to peace;
Ah! do not prize them less, because inspired,

As thou and thine are apt and proud
    to do.
If not inspired, that fragrant page
    had stood,
Time's treasure, and the wonder of
    the wise!
  1681-1765.   —EDWARD YOUNG.

TRIBUTES.
PART II.

THE Bible is like nature, omnivorous, yet healthful. It has a Divine vitality, which enables it to absorb and assimilate elements most diverse and contradictory. Nature is ever clean, healthful, and serene. Though teeming cities may shed their filth upon her bosom, though the malaria may reek, and the earthquake throb here and there, yet she has an exhaustless recuperative, and assimilative energy, which distills perfume from carrion, sweetness from rottenness. So the Bible, with all its contradictory moods, and conflicting statements, is ever infinitely calm and healthful, because infinitely vital. Nature, man, and Scripture, when read with an open eye, prove themselves to be successive volumes on the same theme, and from the same Hand.
—*FALES H. NEWHALL, D. D.*

Part II.

272 IT may be that this last battle of the world is to prove the most terrible of all. Satan is evidently bringing up his reserves, and arming his hosts for the heaviest onset the Church has yet seen. Ancient paganism fell before the Gospel; mediæval superstition gave way before it. But will not these new organizations of evil in which the human heart is displaying its deadliest antipathies to God, prove too strong for it? Will it not have to retire discomfited before those armies of the aliens? No; if this be the last battle, there must out of it come a last victory for the Book of God. Whether that victory may result in a wide acceptance of the Truth over Europe is a question I do not undertake to answer; but that there will be a victory of some kind for the Bible, I believe—victory which will show that there is no amount of antagonism to God which it can not face, and no strength of human evil with which it can not cope successfully as the power of God unto salvation.

1808–1890. —H. Bonar,
"White Fields of France," p. 324,

273 THERE are philosophers of the world—your cosmogonists, or whatever you please to term them—that are boring down to the deepest stratum to frame their hypotheses, their ideas. God forbid that I should hold for a moment true science to be in quarrel with revelation. That can never be. No, sir; the God who made nature wrote the Bible; and I am not prepared to be an infidel as regards the one principle any more than an infidel as regards the other.
—George W. Bethune.

274 THE inspired poetry of David or of Job, the simple narrative of the evangelists, the fiery eloquence of Peter and Paul, are unequaled by any poets or prose-writers of any age or country. And why should they not,

then, educate their students as well as Homer or Virgil?
—MAUD B. BOOTH,
"Beneath Two Flags," p. 249.

275 THAT the Bible is not less conducive to the well-being of man in this life, than it is essential to his hopes in that which is to come, as a theoretical truth might in advance be deduced from the character of the Sacred Volume, the nature of its contents and their adaptation to the character and condition of man, both as an isolated individual and as a member of organized society. As a practical truth it is established by our experience of the past, and is therefore an historical fact; indeed, the course of the sun in the progress of the seasons is not more distinctly marked by its impress on vegetable life than has been the dissemination of the Bible in its influence upon the individual character and the social condition of man. Wherever the Bible has been circulated it has re-

claimed the individual from superstition; has enlightened, purified, and given true direction to that religious principle which seems to be a constituent element in his nature. . . . Still more extensive has been the influence of the Bible upon man's social condition. . . . Wherever it has gone it has carried with it juster notions of individual rights and sounder views of the true end and object of government. It has exerted a great and benign influence upon the enactment of laws and their execution. It has given its solemn sanction to the establishment of right, and has tempered with mercy the administration of justice. And while it has meliorated the punishment of offenses by the introduction and improvement of penitentiary and correctional systems, it has greatly strengthened those of preventive police by imposing its binding restraints upon the indulgence of the passions and the commission of crimes. Equally great and salutary has been the influence of the Bible upon

the mental labors and the intellectual condition of man in all ages and in all countries. It has chastened his imagination and invigorated his judgment. It has purified literature, elevated philosophy, directed science to its true ends and aims, and thus effectually contributed to the advancement of civilization and the melioration of the world.
—Hon. Luther Bradish,
Address before the American Bible Society.
1783–1863.

276 NOT only does the Bible inculcate with sanctions of highest import a system of the purest morality; but in the person and character of our blessed Savior it exhibits a tangible illustration of that system. In him we have set before us—what, till the publication of the Gospel, the world had never seen—a model of feeling and action, adapted to all times, places, and circumstances; and combining so much of wisdom, benev-

olence, and holiness, that none can fathom its sublimity; and yet presented in a form so simple that even a child may be made to understand and taught to love it.

—BENJAMIN F. BUTLER,
In an Address at Alexandria, D C.
1818–1876.

277 THIS Work in all ages of the world has ever met the wants of man, has ever answered the earnest questions of a struggling spirit as no human philosophy ever can. While it offers its truths to those men highly endowed by God, it is emphatically also the poor man's Book, though he may be ignorant of the various arguments to support it. The Scriptures come home to his nature and meet the various wants of his soul, and he finds a basis for belief that the hands of infidelity can never tear down. They bring him comfort in his hours of despondency. Were the Bible removed, the millions of earth would be like mariners upon the stormy ocean without pole-star or compass.

 1817— —JOSEPH CUMMINGS,
  President Wesleyan University.

278 IT is a grand subject for meditation, to behold in our modern societies the love of the holy doctrines of the Gospel advancing with the progress of philosophy and of political institutions, so that the nations which are most advanced in civilization and in liberty are also the most religious, the most truly Christian.

  —BARON DE STAEL (*fils*).

279 WHENCE has sprung this redeeming spirit that has already borne its blessings to every clime; that floats the Bethel flag, penetrates the gloom of the prison; that soothes the orphan's cry, and pleads the cause of the widow; that opens the stores of thought and memory to the long-bound intellects of the deaf and dumb; that is now closing the door of the dram-shop—that broad and

crowded gateway to despair—and is sounding the alarm and concentrating the efforts of the wise and good in view of the Sabbath profanation? The Bible has done all, sir. Seal up this one volume, and in half a century all these hopes would wither and these prospects perish forever. Those sacred temples would crumble or become receptacles of pollution and crime.

—THEODORE FRELINGHUYSEN.
1787-1861.

280 MY present object is to hint at the intimate connection between the Bible and our national prosperity. The destinies of our beloved country are peculiarly associated with the Bible. It was under the auspices of the Bible that our country was settled; it was the Bible that conducted the Pilgrim to our eastern, and the Friend to our central wilderness. If the revolution which made us free differed in mildness of character from all previous revolutions, it was because the Bible mitigated its severity. If

our emancipated country has risen from infancy to vigorous youth, if she is now hailed as the hope of the world, the tyrant's dread, and the patriot's boast, let her thank her statesmen much; let her thank her Bible more. A despotic government may subsist without the Bible; a republic can not. A republic can not, like a despotic government, be sustained by force. She can not, like a despot, tame her children into heartless submission by the bayonets of a mercenary army; her bayonets are reserved for the invading foe. She must depend for domestic tranquillity, for preserving her mild institutions pure and unimpaired, on the wide diffusion of moral principle. Were men angels, they would need no government but the precepts of their Creator. Were they devils, they must be bound in adamantine chains; and as they approximate the one state or the other, their government must be free or must be severe. The patriot then, as well as the Christian, must anxiously inquire, What are the best means of promoting, what the surest foundation of human virtue? . . . The Being who made man has also condescended to propose a plan for his moral improvement; a plan exceeding in effect all human systems as far as the Legislator of the heavens surpasses in wisdom the statesmen of earth. The Bible is not a scheme of abstract faith and doctrine; its great object is to render man virtuous here, and thus prepare him for happiness hereafter. . . . It pervades every department of society, and brings its variegated mass within the influence of that high moral principle which is the only substitute for despotic power. This controlling and sustaining principle has no substantial basis but the Bible; its other foundations have ever proved to be sand. The Bible is found to be its only rock. . . . A republic without the Bible will inevitably become the victim of licentiousness; it contains within itself the turbulent and untamable elements of its own destruction. There is no political Eden for

fallen man save what the Bible protects. —George Griffin,
New York. Address before the American Bible Society.

281 DESPOTISM may exist independent of morality; but republics soon perish when the people becomes corrupt. The efforts of Christian patriots, therefore, must be directed to elevate and sustain the moral character of our citizens; and no method is so efficient to this end as to imbue them with the knowledge and wisdom of the Bible. It opens to our view the only true source of moral obligation or of public and private duty, and enforces these with the only sanctions that can affect the mind and reach the conscience of man; namely, the omniscience and goodness and mercy of God and the certain retributions of the life to come. Without these sanctions, the laws are no longer observed; oaths lose their hold on the conscience; promises are violated; frauds are multiplied, and moral obligation is dissolved. And

these securities natural religion does not furnish; they are found in the Bible alone. In sublimity of thought, in grandeur of conception, in purity and elevation of moral principle, in the practical wisdom of its teachings, and, above all, in the high and important character of its themes, the Holy Bible is not even approached by any human composition.
—SIMON GREENLEAF,
Harvard University School of Law.
1781–1853.

282 WE say, then, that the writings about which there is no dispute amongst Christians, and which have any particular person's name affixed to them are that author's whose title they are marked with, because the first writers quote those books under those names. Neither did any heathens or Jews raise any controversy as if they were not the works of those whose they were said to be. . . . There is no reason for us Christians to doubt the credibility of these

books (of the Old Testament) because there are testimonies in our books (of the New Testament) out of almost every one of them. Nor did Christ, when he reproved many things in the teachers of the Law, ever accuse them of falsifying the books of Moses and the Prophets, or of using supposititious or altered books. And it can never be proved or made creditable that after Christ's time the Scripture should be corrupted in anything of moment, if we do but consider how far and wide the Jewish nation, who everywhere kept these books, was dispersed over the whole world.   Hugo Grotius.
1583–1645.

283 LET this precious Volume have its proper influence on the hearts of men, and our liberties are safe, our country blessed, and the world happy. There is not a tie that unites us to our families, not a virtue that endears us to our country, nor a hope that thrills your bosoms in the prospect of future happiness, that has not **its**

foundation in this Sacred Book. It is the charter of characters—the palladium of liberty—the standard of righteousness. Its Divine influence can soften the heart of the tyrant, can break the rod of the oppressor, and exalt the humblest peasant to the dignified rank of an immortal being, an heir of eternal glory.
—John C. Hornblower,
Chief Justice of New Jersey.

284 NO good for bad white man to tell me the Bible is not true. It stopped my swearin' and stealin' and lyin', when I'd done 'em all forty years steady. It's a miracle that I've stopped, but it would be a bigger one if a book that wa'n't true could 'a' made me." —Indian Convert.

285 HUMAN laws labor under many other great imperfections. They extend to external actions only. They can not reach that catalogue of secret crimes which are committed without any witness save the all-seeing eye of that Being whose presence is

everywhere, and whose laws reach the hidden recesses of vice, and carry their sanctions to the thoughts and intents of the heart. In this view the doctrines of the Bible supply all the deficiencies of human laws, and lend an essential aid to the administration of justice. —JAMES KENT,
1763-1847. Chancellor, New York.

286 MY opinion of the Sacred Volume is, that it is to a nation as the keystone to the arch. No nation can long exist in peace that does not respect it. It carries peace and happiness into every society where its precepts are loved and its commands obeyed. To the young, its value and importance are beyond compare.
—COLONEL LOOMIS,
1852— United States Army.

287 AS the king among his subjects, as the sun among the stars, so is the Bible compared with every other book. . . . It is to this blessed Volume that we are indebted for the gen-

eral temperance, industry, and contentment of the teeming millions of this happy and highly-favored country.
—Joseph Henry Lumpkin,
1812–1860.   Chief Justice, Georgia.

288 THE Book is not the truth; it contains it. The types and words are not the truth or the Word of God; they are but the outward expression and symbols of that Word.
—Charles Pettit McIlvaine,
Bishop Protestant Episcopal Church.
Address at 42d Anniversary American Bible Society.
1799–1873.

289 BUT herein to our Prophets far beneath
As men divinely taught and better teaching
The solid rules of civil government
In their majestic, unaffected style,
Than all the oratory of Greece and Rome.
In them is plainest taught and easiest learnt

What makes a nation happy, and keeps it so,
What ruins kingdoms and lays cities flat.
1608–1674. —JOHN MILTON.

290 NO one can estimate or describe the salutary influences of the Bible. What would the world be without it? Compare the dark places of the earth where the light of the Gospel has not penetrated with those where it has been proclaimed and embraced in all its purity. . . . The Bible has shed a glorious light upon our world. . . The Bible has given us a sublime and pure morality, to which the world was a stranger. . . . No system out of the Bible recognizes an Omniscient Power which scrutinizes the actions of men, and, looking behind the act, takes notice of the motive. . . . The laws

which belong to the social relation are found in the Bible.
> —John McLean,
> Justice of the U. S. Supreme Court.
> 1785-1861.
> On the Wholesome Influence of the Bible on our Social and Civil Life.

291 AS bread accompanies all our meals all through our lives, so ought the reading of the Word of God to accompany all our studies.
> —Jean Frederick Oberlin.
> 1735-1806.

292 I DO declare to the whole world that we believe the Scriptures to contain a declaration of the mind and will of God in and to those ages in which they were written; being given forth by the Holy Ghost, moving in the hearts of holy men of God; that they ought also to be read, believed, and fulfilled in our day; being useful for reproof and inspiration, that

the man of God may be perfect. They are a declaration and testimony of heavenly things, but not the heavenly things themselves, and, as such, we carry a high respect for them. We accept them as the words of God himself; and, by the assistance of his Spirit, they are read with great instruction and comfort.

1644-1718. —WILLIAM PENN.

293 THERE is a saying, as true as it is trite, that we seldom estimate blessings properly until we have lost them; and perhaps, therefore, the vast importance of the Bible, not only to ourselves, but to those unhappy beings who have never known it, may be best imagined and most strongly impressed upon our minds by considering, for a moment, what we ourselves would be without it. Suppose, then, that at this very moment the Bible, with all the institutions connected with it, were blotted from existence, what would be the effect upon this happy and enlightened land? Would it not become comparatively a scene of worse than Egyptian darkness and savage barbarism? Would it not become, compared with what it now is, a melancholy scene of civil, political, and moral degradation; and exhibit the same relation to its present palmy state that is now presented by the pagan and heathen natives of the world? Can there be a doubt of this? Is it not a fact that exactly in proportion as the principles of the Gospel prevail among a people, or they are ignorant of and unactuated by them, so they are either distinguished by all the qualities and endowments that elevate and purify and adorn our nature, or debased by the vices and abominations that degrade it? Is it not a fact that heathen nations generally are the more ignorant and barbarous on the earth; and that while all Christian nations are immeasurably elevated above the heathen in knowledge, virtue, and benevolence, so the relative rank and attainments of Christian uations themselves are governed by the extra degree in which they possess and practice the Gospel in its purity?

—H. L. Pinckney, M. C.,
From South Carolina.
In Address at Bible Meeting, District of Columbia. 1834.

294 IN New Zealand, and in other parts of the world, we are laying the foundation of new societies; and the future character and moral tendency of those societies which may spring up into great kingdoms may be, and no doubt will be, determined by the basis of moral and religious instruction upon which we now establish them. If at their first institution there be no pains taken to instill into their minds the principles of true religion, in place of becoming great and valuable kingdoms, the inhabitants may become pests to all around them, corrupting all within their reach; but if, in laying the foundation of their future empire, we shall sow the truth of real religion, hereafter this land may claim for itself the proud and high distinction of having propagated the knowledge and Word of God, and of having laid the foundation, not only of great, but moral kingdoms.

 1788–1850. —Robert Peel,
  From Address, Tamworth. 1827.

295 MANY and ingenious speculations have been given to the world to account for the repeated and disastrous failure of the successive attempts which have been made, during the last seventy years, to establish and sustain a system of free government in this country. However numerous and various the secondary causes to which the melancholy and remarkable fact may be ascribed, the one efficient and primary cause, I am convinced, is to be found in the general eradication from the national mind of Divine truth and Divine authority by the philosophy, falsely so-called, of the last century, which had its origin and has continued to maintain its fatal influence here. The French nation has not been wanting in many of the circumstances ordinarily deemed the most essential to the practice and support of free government. They have undoubtedly had, in their successive essays at constitutional liberty, the aid and direction of many men of great and distinguished talents, in a worldly sense, both in the cabinet and the senate. Nor are the mass of the people so ignorant and uninformed on general topics as is by some imagined. With the exception of the mere rural laborers, it would be hard to find any country in which the population engaged in the ordinary industrious callings of life are more intelligent, nimble-witted, and even exercised in reading of certain kinds. There is one Book, however, which remains sealed, for the the most part, to all classes of society, and that is the Book of Eternal Wisdom, with all its precious lessons of duty to God and man, of temperance, of moderation, of self-control, of conscientious obedience to the still small voice within. Hence it is that in the agitations and struggles inseparable from the existence of civil and political freedom, abandoned to the infirmities of our common nature, without the chastening discipline of the Gospel, they have had no internal strength to fortify and keep them erect against the disturbing influences from without, and to restrain the violence and fury of the passions; no monitor to recall them, from time to time, from the eagerness of their worldly contentions and pursuits to the recollection of their immortal destinies and responsibilities; no standard of infallible truth by which to try the inventions of mere human reason. And thus have we seen in so many instances, in this country, a fitful and spurious liberty degenerating into license and crime, or torn and distracted by factions, or frightening mankind by the proclamation of new and disorganizing theories, to be swallowed up at last in a degrading and relentless despotism. The lesson which the melancholy experience of France teaches on this subject is one of universal application. The

blessings of a free popular government can not, I am convinced, be long preserved anywhere but by the influence and discipline of the Christian religion deeply implanted in the hearts and lives of all classes of society.
—WILLIAM CABELL RIVES,
1793–1868. United States Minister to France. 1852.
On the Connection Between Civil and Political Liberty and the Study and Reverence of the Holy Scriptures.

296 I HAVE had this Bible as my companion for fifty-three years. Forty-one years of that time I have spent at sea; I have been in forty-five engagements; have been fifteen times wounded, and three times shipwrecked; I have had fevers, of different kinds, fifteen times. But my consolation has always been in this little Companion of mine.
—AN ENGLISH SEAMAN,
On showing a well-worn Bible at the depository of the London Bible Society.

297 WOULD that a history of the American Revolution could have been written by one who, like Xenophon, was a distinguished actor in the scenes described, and who, imbued with the right spirit, could illustrate by appropriate facts the influence which animated and upheld the agents in that mighty struggle! In such a work, if I mistake not, the present and future generations would perceive the fruits of early Biblical instruction, and learn the value of the Bible in the day of adversity. They would see the effect of a mother's early faithfulness to the immortal Washington, who suffered not a day to pass over him without consulting his Bible. They would behold in an American Congress, fully exemplified, the union of humble piety with exalted patriotism; a body on whom the whole conduct of the war was developed, but who, nevertheless, could anxiously deliberate on the means of obtaining from abroad (such was their estimate of its worth) copies of the Sacred

Volume for their destitute and imploring fellow-citizens; in short, they would perceive, not only the gallant bearing of a patriot army, but their patient endurance under unparalleled privations, and the invincible spirit displayed by all classes of a suffering people plainly ascribable, in no moderate degree, to an early and deeply-impressed acquaintance with the Bible through the medium of maternal faithfulness and the common school.
—JOHN COTTON SMITH.
1765–1845.

298 HERE, then, the body of educated men must take their stand. By all the means in their power they must endeavor to avert the pestilent mischief of desecrating the places of instruction, of separating the culture of the heart from that of the mind, and under the pretense of a liberal morality that is clear in its source, pure in its precepts, and efficacious in its influence—*the morality of the Gospel.* —JOHN SARGENT,
Address Nassau Hall.

299 THE antiquary will return, with no ordinary curiosity, to the earliest complete volume that remains to us of ancient manuscript, and the first that issued from the press after the invention of printing. The historian, if he regards it of no higher authority than Herodotus, will prize it as the precursor of that author and the foundation of his department. The statesman will face the outlines of the earliest legislation and jurisprudence known to history, and the most perfect moral code of any age or country. The lawyer, in the details of the professional pursuits which engage his attention through life, will meet with many pertinent examples and instructions. —DAVID SWAIN,
1801–1868. Governor North Carolina.

300 THE Scriptures also teach that to derive all the benefit which God designed to bestow in revealing himself to his fallen creatures, man, on his part, must strive to do God's will. Let man do this, and he will know whether the Bible is the Word of God

or a cunningly devised fable. Men of any experience and observation must have seen those who have been reclaimed from a profane and immoral course of conduct to sobriety, truth, piety, and happiness, by studying and obeying the Sacred Oracles of eternal truth. —Commodore Skinner,
United States Navy. 1852.

301 THE Bible is the grand charter of man's political and civil equality, liberty, and order. It is the guardian and the only adequate protector of his social happiness. Should the human race ever come fully under its influence, both national wars and personal dissensions would cease, and this world would become a terrestrial paradise.
—Benjamin Silliman, Sr.,
1779-1864. Yale College.

302 OF all men, American scholars ought not to be ignorant of anything which the Bible contains. If Cicero could declare that the laws of the twelve tables were worth all the

libraries of the philosophers; if they were the *carmen necessarium* of the Roman youth, — how laboriously ought you to investigate its contents, and inscribe them upon your hearts!
—Samuel Lewis Southard,
1787–1842.   Governor of New Jersey.

303 IF there be any one subject that at this day commands general attention, it is that of national and social oppression. This is not confined to one country or one people, but it is so throughout all Christendom. Humanity everywhere rises up and denies the law of its bondage. . . . How were the American people electrified by the masses of Europe linking together in one brotherhood, the high and the low, under impulses common to our nature! All this we saw with amazement and delight, and then we beheld the ground, so nobly won, all lost. Despotism and treachery decimated and crushed the forces of the free. Why was this? We changed our form of government, and peace and quiet followed. They made

the same attempt, and failed. The cause did not exist in mere outward circumstances, but in the want of those early associations derived from the Word of God. A free Bible makes free men the world over. Without Bible views of liberty and equality, the American Revolution would have been smothered in its own blood. . . . We hear much of the mission of the American people. One mission, at least, we have; but it should be understood that our success lies, not in outward constitutions, but in those inner principles that are the seeds of a Christian democracy. Constitutions and charters are all well, but they must have their basis in that great charter given by the King Eternal, immortal, and invisible, as a foundation on which to erect the superstructure of human rights. The late-lamented Legare said that every man who stepped from the *Mayflower* was himself a living constitution; and until Europe posseses such men she will pant for liberty in vain. We can be liberty-propagandists only by becoming Bible-propagandists. Carlyle may write his latter-day pamphlets to try to stay the progress of democracy, but here, in the Bible, is the great latter-day pamphlet which will survive that great day for which all other days were made. It needs no eulogy. Christianity has written it on the whole course of her history.

—JOHN THOMPSON,
> In an Address to the theme: The Bible, in its letter and spirit, furnishes the best of all standards by which to test the numerous theories of the day for improving the condition and prospects of the race.

304 I ACCEPT, with gratitude and pleasure, your gift of this inestimable Volume. It was for the love of the truths of this great and good Book that our fathers abandoned their native shores for the wilderness. Animated by its lofty principles, they toiled and suffered till the desert blossomed as the rose. These same truths sustained them in their resolution to become a free nation; and,

guided by the wisdom of this Book, they founded a government under which we have grown from three millions to more than twenty millions of people, and from being but a stock on the borders of this continent, we have spread from the Atlantic to the Pacific. —ZACHARY TAYLOR,
1784–1850. 12th President of the U. S. To the ladies of Frankfort, on receiving a copy of the Bible bound with that of the Constitution of the United States.

305 BY government, we are to understand the power that makes and administers law. Every government has certain duties to discharge; foremost among which is the restraint of the passions of man, the repression of turbulence and disorder, and this is the direct object of a police. The necessity for such action grows out of the universal prevalence of passions that need to be repressed. The form of this police depends upon the genius of the people who are governed. In a despotic nation it is very simple, consisting merely in the exercise of

terror and of force. So in decayed and false republics, like that of Venice, the police has a secret and unbounded power. But in such a country as ours the problem is one not so easily solved. Yet here, it must be manifest that a vigilant and effective police is absolutely necessary to the prevalence of order and of quiet. The liberty of speech and opinion which prevails renders this essential, and to accomplish this object we must look to something more than the array of civil officers. There is little in our form of government to inspire awe or fear; it operates silently and almost unnoticed. We must have other and stronger support than the array of authority finds. And although the intelligence of the people is one great element of this reliance, still to the Bible, and to the power of the truths which it contains, are we far more indebted than to any other cause for the preservation of order and of peace throughout the land. Even this city, with a vastly increased police, without the Bible, without the pulpit, without any of the influences that flow from the power of religious truth, could not preserve peace and order and security of person and property, for a single year. The Bible makes a man afraid to do wrong, because it teaches him that he thereby violates the laws of his conscience and his God. And by this influence alone it contributes immensely to the peace and good order of the community. The Bible, moreover, infuses into the bosom of every man a feeling of self-control, and in so doing it lays the foundation for a simple, thorough, and effective government of the country. The cheapness of this method of police, moreover, should commend it to the favor of this money-loving age. In all respects it is infinitely superior to every measure of secret espionage to which a Napoleon or a Nicholas may resort. The elements of such a moral police, it is evident, must be everywhere diffused; must pervade all classes, purify all motives, and inspire everywhere a regard for justice and for the high and holy truths of the Word of

God. To accomplish this, the Bible must find its way into every family and every school-house in the country. Nothing short of this will insure success. Men must be fed, and fed abundantly, with the Bread of Life.
1800–1877. —Emory Washburn,
Governor of Massachusetts.

Speaking to the theme: The general diffusion of the Holy Scriptures, as an efficient measure of domestic police in a republic, deserves the countenance and support of every friend of our free institutions.

306 I REGRET that my time is not more at my command, that I might evince the interest I feel in the Bible-cause by something of more account than mere profession. It is delightful to witness the exertions that are now making by the Christian world to dispel the night of ignorance that yet obscures so large a portion of this

planet, and to supply its place by the light of the cross. The manifestations of Divine support are well-fitted to awaken all our energies and excite us to higher efforts than have ever yet been made. Even if we should not succeed to the full extent of our hopes and wishes, we shall make such an impression as shall shake the heathen world and prepare the way for a complete victory by those who are to follow us. Nay, even if we fail in a great attempt, and the grandeur and philanthropy of the enterprise must be reward enough for all our exertions. But we shall not fail. There is a God who looks down upon us and witnesses our efforts, and a Savior who approves and will sustain us by his intercession. The cause is good, the hearts that support it are true and good, and the God who upholds it is almighty. Let us go on, then, with courage and constancy, nothing doubting, and the Red Sea will open before us, the Rock in the desert will pour forth its stream, and the Eastern wilderness

will once more bud and blossom like the rose. —WILLIAM WIRT,
1772–1834.
Attorney-General, United States.
From a letter addressed, in 1838, to a meeting in New York, the design of which was to increase the circulation of the Scriptures throughout the world.

307 READ the Bible! Read the Bible! Let no religious book take its place. Through all my perplexities and distresses I never read any other book, and I never felt the want of any other. It has been my hourly study; and all my knowledge of the doctrines, and all my acquaintance with the experience and realities of religion, have been derived from the Bible only. I think religious people do not read the Bible enough. Books about religion may be useful enough, but they will not do instead of the simple truth of the Bible.
—WILLIAM WILBERFORCE.
1789–1833.   His dying words.

308 TO those who have carefully observed or considered the progress of civil and religious freedom at different times and in various countries, it can be hardly necessary to say, it has always been the most rapid as well as the most healthy where the Bible was most widely disseminated, and where the sacred truths contained therein were brought home to the greatest number of the people. Indeed, there is no nation, although nominally civilized and Christianized, which has made any very great advancement in the amelioration and improvement of the social condition of the masses except those nations where the Sacred Scriptures were in the hands of and studied by the people generally.
—REUBEN HENRY WALWORTH,
1789–1867.   Chancellor, New York.

309 I SHALL, however, as being in duty bound to follow the truth so far as I can discern it, have to make many confessions to the prejudice, not, as I trust, of Christian belief or of the

Sacred Volume, but only of us who, as its students, have failed gravely and at many points in the duty of a temperate and cautious treatment of it, as unhappily we have also failed in every other duty. But as the lines and laws of duty at large remain unobscured, notwithstanding the imperfections everywhere diffused, so we may trust that sufficient light yet remains for us, if duly followed, whereby to establish the authority and sufficiency of Holy Scripture for its high moral and spiritual purposes. For the present I have endeavored to point out that the operations of criticism, properly so-called, affecting as they do the library form of the books, leave the questions of history, miracle, revelation, substantially where they found them. I shall in several succeeding papers strive to show, at least by specimens, that science and research have done much to sustain the historical credit of the Old Testament; that in doing this they have added strength to the argument which contends that in them we find a Divine revelation; and that the evidence, rationally viewed, both of contents and of results, binds us to stand where our forefathers have stood, upon the IMPREGNABLE ROCK OF HOLY SCRIPTURE.

—WILLIAM EWART GLADSTONE,
"The Impregnable Rock of Holy Scripture."
1809—

INDEXES.

GOOD and holy men and the best and wisest of mankind, the kingly spirits of history, have borne witness to its (the Bible's) influences, and have declared it to be beyond compare the most perfect instrument, the only adequate organ of humanity.
　—*SAMUEL TAYLOR COLERIDGE.*
Confessions of an Inquiring Spirit, p. 71. London, 1840.

GENERAL INDEX.

Arnold, Matthew.........................1, 2, 3
Addison, Joseph............................4
Augustine, St..............................5
Adams, John................................6
Adams, John Quincy...................7, 8, 9
Alexander, I, Czar........................10
Ames, Fisher..............................11
Arbuthnot, Alexander......................12
Anonymous.........................13, 17, 20
Abbott, Lyman.............................14
Ad Fidem (F. E. Burr)...................15
Atterbury, Francis........................16
Arrowsmith, John..........................18
Alexander, Archibald,.....................19

Bunsen, Chevalier.........................21
Beattie, James............................22
Bengal, J. A..............................23
Bartol, C. A..............................24
Bruce, Michael............................25
Brown, J..................................26
Berridge..................................27
Bushe, Chief Justice......................28
Bellows, Henry W..........................29
Briggs, Charles A.........................30
Beard, Dr.............................31, 32
Beecher, Henry Ward...................33, 34
Bishop Boone's Assistant..................35
Billings, Josh............................36
Bacon, Lord...............................37
Boyle, Robert...............38, 39, 40, 41, 42
Bonar, H.................................272
Bethune, George W........................273
Booth, Maud B............................274

Bradish, Luther................................275
Butler, Benjamin F..........................276

Cowper, William......................43, 44, 45
Clarke, James Freeman.....................46
Channing, William Ellery.................47, 48
Coleridge, Samuel Taylor.........49, 50, 51, 52
Clinton, De Witt............................53
Clark, Samuel...............................54
Cheever, George B..........................55
Cecil, Richard..........................56, 57
Cass, Lewis.................................58
Collins, William 59
Carlyle, Thomas.................60, 61, 62, 63
Caine, Hall 64
Clulow, W. B................................65
Conway, M. D................................66
Cummings, Joseph...........................277

Dryden, John.............................67, 68
De Tocqueville, Charles Henry...............69
Dwight, Timothy.............................70
Dana, James Dwight......................71, 72
Dawson, Chancellor..........................73
Diderot, Denis..............................74
D'Aubigne, Merle............................75
Depew, Chauncy M............................76
Dana, Charles A.............................77
De Staël, Baron, *fils*....................278

Ewald, G. H. A..............................78
Emerson, Ralph Waldo........................79
Edward VI...................................80
Everett, Edward.............................81
Ebers, Georg................................82
Evans, Professor L. J...............83, 84, 85
Ecce Deus (Joseph Parker)...................86

Franklin, Benjamin...................87, 88
Flavel, J.................................89
Fawcett, John...........................90
Field, Eugene 91
Faber, F. W.............................92
Froude, James Anthony....................93
Frelinghuysen, Theodore.................279

Gregory I, The Great.....................94
Gilfillan, George....................95, 96
Guizot, F. P. G.........................97
Grant, U. S.............................98
Garibaldi 99
Gladstone, W. E.............100, 101, 309
Greeley, Horace........................102
Goethe, J. W. von.......103, 104, 105, 106
Gibbons, Cardinal......................107
Guyot, A. H............................108
Gladden, Washington....................109
Griffin, George........................280
Greenleaf, Simon.......................281
Grotius, Hugo..........................282

Herbert, George...................110, 111
Howells, R.............................112
Hopkins, Mark..........................113
Hervey, James..........................114
Hall, John.............................115
Hamilton, James...................116, 117
Horsley, Samuel........................118
Huxley, Professor..........119, 120, 121
Hoare, Canon...........................122
Humboldt, Baron........................123
Holland, J. G..........................124
Hornblower, John C.....................283
Harris, John...........................125
Hallam, Henry..........................126

Hooker, Richard..........................127
Heine, Heinrich.....................128, 129
Hervey, Lord Arthur......................130
Hall, Robert 131
Herschel, Sir John.......................132
Hale, Edward Everett....................133
Hugo, Victor............................134

Indian Convert..........................284

Jay, John, Chief Justice..................135
Jackson, Andrew.........................136
Jefferson, Thomas.......................137
Jones, Sir William.......................138
Joubert, F..............................139
Johnson, Samuel.........................140
Jewell, John............................141

Kempis, Thomas á........................142
Kent, Chancellor James.............143, 285
Kitto, John.............................144

Lincoln, A..............................145
Lee, Robert E...........................146
Liddon, Canon...........................147
Levy, Rabbi J. Leonard..................148
Landor, Walter Savage...................149
Lange, J. P.............................150
Locke, John........................151, 152
Lightfoot, J. B.........................153
Loomis, Colonel.........................286
Lumpkin, Joseph Henry..................287
Leask, William....................154, 155, 156
Milton, John.....................157, 158, 289
Macaulay, Lord....................159, 160
Melville, Henry...................161, 162
Mitchell, O. M..........................163

General Index.

Morris, H. W.................................164
McCheyne, Robert M......................165
Maury, Lieutenant..........................166
Murphy, Professor..........................167
Muller, George...............................168
Miller, Hugh..................................169
Munger, Theodore T.......................170
Mitchell, Donald G.........................171
McIlvaine, Charles P......................288
McLain, John.................................290

Newton, Sir Isaac....................172, 173
Novalis (von Hardenberg).................174
Nichol, R. B...................................175
Nott, Eliphalet...............................176
Napoleon I....................177, 178, 179, 180

Oliphant, Mrs.................................181
Oberlin, Jean Frederick....................291

Pope, Alexander.............................182
Payson, Edward.......................183, 184
Phillips, Wendell............................185
Pollok, Robert.........................186, 187, 188
Parker, Theodore.....................189, 190, 191
Pellico, Silvio................................192
Pedro, Emperor Dom......................193
Porteus, Bishop.............................194
Penn, William................................292
Pinckney, H. L..............................293
Porter, Noah..................................195
Parker, Joseph..............................196
Peel, Robert..................................294
Peabody, A. P...............................197
Plenary Council.............................198

Quarles, Francis............................199

General Index.

Rousseau, Jean Jacques..............200, 201
Rochester, Earl of......................202
Rush, Benjamin........................203
Romaine, William......................204
Robertson, Frederick W................205
Rodgers, Henry..............206, 207, 208
Ruskin, John.........209, 210, 211, 212, 213
Rives, William C......................295

Steele, Anne..........................214
Stier, Rudolph........................215
Stanley, A. P.........................216
Stalker, James........................217
Seward, William H.....................218
Spurgeon, Charles H...................219
Steele................................220
Sun, New York.......................221
Simpson, Matthew......................222
Selden, John..........................223
Schaff, Philip........................224
Swift, Dean...........................225*
Story, Chief Justice..................226
Skinner, Commodore....................300
Stillman, B. Sr.......................301
Southard, Samuel I....................302
Sargeant, John........................298
Stephanus, Henry......................227
Smyth, Newman.........................228
Smith, Vance..........................229
Storrs, Richard S...............230, 231
Scott, Sir Walter........232, 233, 234, 235
Swain, David..........................299
Shaftesbury, Earl of.........236, 237, 238
Seaman, An English....................296
Smith, John...........................297
Tennyson, Alfred......................239
Tillotson, Archbishop.................240
Taylor, Isaac...................241, 242

General Index.

Thomson, Edward..........................243
Trail, W...................................244
Taylor, W. M..............................245
Thompson, John............................303
Taylor, Zachary...........................304
Transcript, Boston *Evening*...............246
Tribune, New York........................247
Times, London...........................248
Taylor, Bayard............................249

Van Dyke, H. J............................250

Webster, Daniel..251, 252, 253, 254, 255, 256, 257
World, Christian..........................258
Watson, T.................................259
Wayland, Francis..........................260
Whittier, John G 261
Wright, Wiliam............................262
Watts, Isaac..............................263
Watson, Richard...........................264
Whichcote, Benjamin.......................265
Wallace, Alexander........................266
Winthrop, R. C............................267
Wordsworth, Bishop........................263
Wilson, John..............................264
William, Emperor..........................270
Washburn, Emory...........................305
Wirt, William.............................306

Wilberforce, William......................307
Walworth, R. H............................308

Young, Edward.............................271

TOPICAL INDEX.

Antiquity, 144, 181, 194, 240, 299.
Authenticity and Integrity, 172, 242, 282, 309.
Authority, Supreme, 226.
All, Bible for, 51, 66, 74, 76, 94, 100, 115, 119, 120, 134, 143, 147, 189, 191, 277.
Accuracy, Historical, 18, 28, 82, 130, 172.

Circulation, Advantages of General, 306.
Civilization, The Bible and, 52, 106, 131, 148, 191, 213, 217, 218, 247, 275, 278, 290, 293, 301, 308.
Character, Effect upon, 7, 14, 16, 23, 25, 26, 30, 33, 39, 53, 129, 140, 162, 175, 176, 192, 214, 215, 218, 240, 284, 296, 300.
Criticism, Higher, and Infidelity, 75, 83, 96, 124, 206, 217, 228, 247, 250, 262.
Christ, Bible and, 48, 133, 204, 257, 276.
Classics, Bible and, 263, 264, 274.

Devotion, Bible Means of, and Aid to, 40, 113, 168, 229, 231.
Duty of Giving Attention, 107, 187, 198.

Excellence, General, 6, 8, 10, 20, 22, 31, 38, 41, 43, 44, 57, 59, 60, 62, 78, 90, 110, 111, 112, 114, 128, 138, 139, 145, 146, 152, 157, 165, 173, 174, 185, 187, 191, 201, 205, 214, 222, 224, 233, 234, 235, 241, 244, 254, 259, 261, 271.
Examined, Spirit in which should be, 45.
Exploration, Bible and, 164, 248.

Faith in and Respect for, 36, 97, 103, 104, 221.

History, The Philosophy of, 170, 179.

Inexhaustible, 116, 122, 125, 232.
Imperishable, 15, 17, 24, 34, 95, 141, 154, 190, 207, 237, 238, 272, 291.

Interpretation, 195, 255.
Indispensable, 1, 9, 12, 55, 80, 87, 91, 101, 150, 184, 270, 302.

Liberty, The State and Personal, 21, 37, 58, 69, 81, 86, 88, 98, 99, 102, 136, 137, 143 203, 256, 260, 294.

Morality, Public and Private, 153, 161, 177, 216, 236, 284, 287, 290, 298.
Mystery, Not to be Rejected on account of, 155.

Nature and Providence, Likeness of Bible to, 57, 71, 72, 75, 273.
National Life, 280, 281, 283, 286, 289, 294, 295, 297, 301, 303, 304.

Philanthropy, 279.
Practical and Efficient, 42, 120, 122, 126, 131, 146, 153, 204, 213, 218, 244, 257, 270, 271, 277, 284.

Revelation, The Bible an Inspired, 19, 29, 35, 44, 48, 49, 54, 67, 84, 105, 108, 126, 167, 178, 188, 196, 208, 220, 230, 292.
Reading, Daily, 168, 180, 193, 198, 204, 251, 252.

Science and the Bible, 132, 163, 166, 169, 273.
Self-evidencing Power, 300.
Style, Literary, Effect of Bible on, 11, 32, 50, 65, 64, 68, 77, 85, 91, 92, 93, 121, 123, 149, 157, 158, 159, 160, 171, 182, 197, 209, 210, 211, 212, 213, 220, 225, 227, 243, 246, 248, 253, 268, 274.
Sufficiency of the Bible, 135, 151, 306.

Variety, 156.

Writings, Other Sacred, and the Bible, 46, 109, 182.

INDEX BY PROFESSIONS.

Anonymous, 13, 17, 20.

Clergymen, 5, 14, 15, 24, 26, 29, 30, 31, 32, 33, 34, 38, 39, 40, 41, 42, 46, 47, 48, 54, 55, 56, 57, 86, 89, 90, 92, 94, 107, 109, 114, 115, 116, 117, 118, 122, 125, 127, 131, 141, 142, 147, 148, 153, 154, 155, 156, 168, 170, 176, 183, 184, 194, 196, 204, 205, 216, 217, 219, 222, 225, 228, 230, 231, 240, 243, 244, 245, 259, 262, 263, 264, 265, 268, 272, 273, 288, 291.

Commentators, 14, 23, 144, 150, 167, 215, 282.
Converts from Heathenism, 35, 284.
College Presidents and Professors, 30, 70, 71, 72, 83, 84, 85, 113, 195, 197, 224, 260, 281, 299, 301.
Commanders in Army and Navy, 58, 98, 99, 136, 146, 163, 276, 286, 300.

Evangelist, 274, 300.
Historians, 75, 78, 82, 93, 97, 108, 126.

Infidels, 74, 128, 129, 200, 201, 202.

Journalists, 36, 77, 102.
Jurists, 28, 135, 143, 226, 283, 287, 290.

Literary Critics and Essayists, 1, 2, 3, 60, 61, 62, 63, 69, 79, 91, 95, 96, 124, 130, 133, 140, 149, 159, 160, 164, 171, 174, 181, 206, 207, 208, 209, 210, 211, 212, 213, 249, 269.
Layman, 280, 303.
Liberal Thinkers, 24, 46, 47, 48, 66, 189, 190, 191.

Novelists, 64, 82, 134.
Newspapers, 221, 246, 247, 248, 258.

Orators, 76, 81, 185.
Orientalists, 138.

188

Index by Professions.

Poets, 4, 12, 22, 43, 44, 45, 49, 50, 51, 52, 59, 67, 68, 79, 103, 104, 105, 106, 110, 111, 128, 129, 139, 157, 158, 165, 174, 182, 186, 187, 188, 199, 214, 232, 233, 234, 235, 239, 250, 261, 271, 289.

Philosophers, 37, 151, 152, 172, 173.

Philanthropists, 306.

Physician, 203.

Rulers, 6, 7, 8, 9, 10, 80, 98, 136, 137, 145, 177, 178, 179, 180, 193, 270.

Statesmen, 6, 7, 8, 9, 11, 58, 87, 88, 100, 101, 218, 236, 237, 238, 251, 252, 253, 254, 255, 256, 257, 275, 279, 292, 293, 294, 295, 297, 298, 299, 302, 304, 305, 307, 308.

Scientists, 21, 71, 72, 119, 120, 121, 123, 132, 163, 166, 169.

INDEX BY NATIONALITY.

Great Britian, 1, 2, 3, 4, 12, 16, 18, 19, 22, 25, 26, 27, 37, 38, 43, 44, 45, 49, 50, 51, 52, 56, 57, 59, 60, 61, 62, 63, 64, 67, 68, 80, 86, 89, 90, 92, 93, 95, 96, 100, 101, 110, 111, 114, 116, 117, 118, 119, 120, 121, 122, 126, 127, 130, 131, 132, 138, 140, 141, 144, 145, 146, 149, 151, 152, 153, 154, 155, 156, 157, 158, 159, 160, 161, 162, 168, 169, 172, 173, 181, 182, 186, 187, 188, 194, 196, 202, 204, 205, 209, 210, 211, 212, 213, 214, 216, 217, 219, 223, 225, 229, 232, 233, 234, 235, 236, 237, 238, 239, 240, 241, 242, 244, 248, 259, 263, 264, 265, 266, 268, 269, 271, 272, 274, 289, 294, 296, 307, 309.

America, 6, 7, 8, 9, 11, 14, 15, 24, 28, 29, 30, 33, 34, 46, 47, 48, 53, 55, 58, 66, 70, 71, 72, 76, 77, 79, 81, 83, 84, 85, 87, 88, 91, 98, 102, 107, 109, 113, 115, 124, 133, 135, 136, 137, 143, 147, 148, 163, 164, 166, 170, 171, 176, 183, 184, 185, 189, 190, 191, 195, 197, 198, 203, 218, 221, 222, 224, 226, 228, 230, 231, 243, 245, 246, 247, 249, 251, 252, 253, 254, 255, 256, 257, 258, 260, 261, 262, 273, 275, 276, 277, 279, 280, 281, 283, 284, 286, 287, 288, 290, 292, 293, 295, 297, 298, 299, 300, 301, 302, 303, 304, 305, 306, 308.

Russia, 10.

France, 69, 74, 97, 134, 139, 177, 178, 179, 180, 200, 201, 278.

Germany, 21, 22, 78, 82, 103, 104, 105, 106, 123, 128, 129, 150, 215, 270, 291.

Holland, 282.

Brazil, 193.

Switerland, 75, 108.

Italy, 94, 99.

APPENDIX.

ONE of the most thrilling incidents in the War of 1812 was the bombardment of Fort McHenry. As darkness settled down, it left our flag still floating. The night was made hideous by the glare of " bombs bursting in air." Anxiety drove sleep from the eyes of patriots. They yearned for the morning, and yet dreaded its revelation. But when the dawn came, they beheld with joy that the " flag was still there"—the fort had withstood its foes! There stands the Bible, the citadel of our faith. Enemies open upon it their broadsides. Sometimes Christians almost despair. But when the smoke rolls away, though beneath its ramparts is piled the débris of human opinions, there stands the Bible, and, floating serenely from the outer wall, the banner, bearing this device : " The gates of hell shall not prevail against it."   DR. DAVID H. MOORE.

THE INTERNATIONAL BIBLE-LESSON SYSTEM.

IT is significant that a business man and a bishop* share the laurel wreath as inaugurators of the International System of Uniform Bible Lessons. When the idea was first proposed in the National Sunday-school Convention, at Indianapolis, 1872, a delegate characterized it as impracticable. In illustration, he told of Jeferson's saw-mill, *on top of a mountain:* "A good enough saw-mill, *but how were the logs to be gotten up to it?*" Well, the logs have come to the mill. The system is a triumphant success. Evangelical denominations of Christendom, with but small exception, have adopted it. The scheme is affecting deeply, and in a salutary manner, our current Christian life. It is

---
*B. F. Jacobs, Esq., and Bishop John H. Vincent.

producing some blessed phenomena; notably, practical Christian unity, a prodigious and excellent Bible-literature, and such general and thorough study of the blessed Word as the world has never seen before.

A few figures show the wideness of the influence of this system, now beginning the second quarter-century of its history.

The International Lessons are now practically adopted by the Sunday-school world, in which, according to the last census, there were 218,562 schools, 2,229,728 officers and teachers, and 20,168,933 scholars.* In the United States, enough teachers' helps upon the current lessons are published to supply each of the million teachers with two of different kinds; and of scholars' helps, one each to 8,500,000. The aggregate of leaflets is 485,000,000 copies *per annum*.† The aggregate circulation of evangelical weekly papers

---

* Last World's Sunday-school Convention, St. Louis, 1893.

† Seventh International Sunday-school Convention, St. Louis, 1893.

Appendix. 195

is 2,479,000 per annum.* Almost without exception, these periodicals devote some space, more or less, to the current lesson. An increasing number of secular newspapers, daily and weekly, are doing the same.

---

*Evan's Standard List of Evangelical Periodicals.

THE BIBLE SOCIETIES AND THE DIFFUSION OF THE WORD.

SEVERAL Bible Societies were in evidence in Europe before the opening of this century. They were, however, limited in resources and sphere of operation. In 1804 the British and Foreign Bible Society was founded. It has proved "the greatest agency for the diffusion of the Word of God." In its first ninety-two years it distributed 147,366,669 copies. In the making of translations and versions for use in mission-fields, and donations to the same, printing, binding, colportage, and general administration, the princely sum of over $50,000,000 has been expended by this Society since its inception.

The American Bible Society, the next greatest association of this kind, was organized in 1816. In the first eighty years of its history it distributed 61,705,841 copies in about one hundred languages and dialects.

There are upwards of seventy other Bible Societies in the world, besides several thousand Auxiliary Societies. It is estimated that their aggregate issues, previous to April, 1897, amount to more than 257,000,000 copies. F. M. Rains asserts that the Bible is now translated into a sufficient number of languages to make it accessible to nine-tenths of the inhabitants of the world.

IGNORANCE RESPECTING THE BIBLE.

THE Bible is studied in a certain one of our colleges one hour a week during the larger part of the four years of the course. At the first exercise of the years 1894–95 of the freshman class, I determined to gather up evidence as to what the men knew of the Bible. At this first recitation, thirty-four men were present. On the blackboard of the room I wrote out twenty-two extracts from Tennyson. Each of these extracts had an allusion to some Scriptural scene or truth. Each man was provided with paper, and was asked to explain each allusion. The twenty-two selections which were made are as follows:

"My sin was a thorn
Among the thorns that girt Thy brow."
—"*Supposed Confessions.*"
"As manna on my wilderness."—*Ibid.*

Appendix.

"That God would move,
And strike the hard, hard rock, and thence,
Sweet in their utmost bitterness,
Would issue tears of penitence."—*Ibid.*

"Like that strange angel which of old
Until the breaking of the light
Wrestled with wandering Israel."
—"*To——*"

"Like Hezekiah's, backward runs
The shadow of my days."
—"*Will Waterproof.*"

"Joshua's moon in Ajalon."
—"*Locksley Hall.*"

"A heart as rough as Esau's hand."
—"*Godiva.*"

"Gash thyself, priest, and honor thy brute
Baal." —"*Alymer's Field.*"

"Ruth amid the fields of corn."—*Ibid.*

"Pharaoh's darkness."—*Ibid.*

"A Jonah's gourd
Up in one night, and due to sudden sun."
—"*The Princess.*"

"Stiff as Lot's wife."—*Ibid.*

"Arimathæan Joseph."—"*The Holy Grail.*"

"For I have flung thee pearls, and find thee
swine." —*The Last Tournament.*"

"Perhaps, like him of Cana in Holy Writ,
Our Arthur kept his best until the last."
—"*The Holy Grail.*"

"And marked me even as Cain."
—"*Queen Mary.*"

"The Church on Peter's Rock."—*Ibid.*

"Let her eat dust like the serpent, and be driven out of her Paradise."
—"*Becket.*"

"A whole Peter's sheet."—*Ibid.*

"The godless Jephtha vows his child. . . . To one cast of the dice."
—"*Early Spring.*"

"A Jacob's ladder falls."—"*The Flight.*"

"Follow Light and do the Right—for man can half control his doom—
Till you find the deathless Angel seated in the vacant tomb."
—"*Locksley Hall, Sixty Years After.*"

It is to be noticed that the allusions contained in these extracts are not at all recondite; one might, indeed, have chosen selections which do contain recondite illusions. For instance, one might have asked the class to explain this line, taken from "The Palace of Art:"

"One was the Tishbite whom the raven fed."

Or one might have taken these lines from "A Dream of Fair Women:"

"Moreover it is written that my race
Hewed Ammon hip and thigh from Aroer
On Arnon unto Minnith."

But the allusions that were selected are of the more common sort.

And now let me ask, Who and what were the men who were asked to explain these allusions? They were young men of about twenty years of age, born in the northern part of Ohio, or in the central part of New York State, or in Western Pennsylvania. Every one was born in this country excepting one, who was born in London. They were the sons of lawyers, preachers, teachers, merchants, and farmers. Every one, except one, expressed himself as holding an ecclesiastical affiliation, and more than half were associated with two Churches which are supposed specially to represent an intelligent knowledge of the Bible. Of the number, nine were Congregationalists and Presbyterians each, five were Methodist, three were Baptists, two were of the Reformed Church, two were Jews, and one each belonged to the Free Baptist, the Unitarian, and the Roman Catholic Churches, and one, as has been said, indicated no ecclesiastical relation.

And what did the men thus born and bred and trained know of the Scriptural scenes and truths expressed in these verses of Tennyson? I venture to give the record just as it stands. Nine failed to understand the quotation:

"My sin was a thorn
Among the thorns that girt Thy brow."

Eleven failed to apprehend the "manna on my wilderness." Sixteen were likewise ignorant of the significance of striking the rock. Sixteen, also, knew nothing about the wrestling of Jacob and the angel. No less than thirty-two had never heard of the shadow turning back on the dial for Hezekiah's lengthening life. Twenty-six were ignorant of "Joshua's moon." Nineteen failed to indicate the peculiar condition of Esau's hand. Twenty-two were unable to explain the allusion to Baal. Nineteen had apparently never read the idyl of Ruth and Boaz. Eighteen failed to indicate the meaning of

"Pharaoh's darkness. Twenty-eight were laid low by the question about Jonah's gourd. Nine, and nine only, were unable to explain the allusion to Lot's wife. Twenty-three did not understand who "Arimathæan Joseph" was. Twenty-two, also, had not read the words of Christ sufficiently to explain, "For I have flung thee pearls and find thee swine." Twenty-four had apparently not so read the account of Christ's first miracle as to be able to explain the reference. Eleven did not understand the mark which Cain bore. Twenty-five were as ignorant as a heathen of the foundation of the Church on Peter. Twelve, and twelve only, had not gathered up knowledge sufficient to indicate certain truths about the serpent in Eden. No less then twenty-seven were paralyzed by the allusion, "A whole Peter's sheet." Twenty-four were unable to write anything as to Jephtha's vow. Eleven only, however, were struck dumb by the allusion to Jacob's ladder. But sixteen were able to write a proper explanation of "the deathless angel seated in the vacant tomb." In a word, to each of these thirty-four men, twenty-two questions were put, which would demand seven hundred and forty-eight answers. The record shows that out of a possible seven hundred and forty-eight correct answers, only three hundred and twenty-eight were given.—*"A College President," in the Independent.*

THE BIBLE AS A TEXT-BOOK.

AS the chairman of the Committee of the American Society of Religious Education — one of whose aims it is to increase the study of the Bible—on the subject of "The Bible in College and University," about the last of October and the first of November, 1895, I issued seventy-one circulars, propounding the following questions:

"1. Is the Bible used as a text-book in your institution? If so, please state how much time is given.

"2. Are there any organized Bible-reading classes among your students?

"3. Is the interest in the Bible among your students on the increase?

"4. Can you make any helpful or stimulating suggestions by which to increase the interest of college students in the Bible?

"5. Are you willing to co-operate in an effort in behalf of the Bible in the college?

"6. Can our Society assist you on this matter in any way?"

I received forty-one answers, mostly immediate, and from the hand of the presidents of the institutions addressed. The following is the substance of the replies from some of the New England colleges.

President Andrews, Brown University:

"In Brown, the Bible is the basis of eleven courses of study, each covering three hours a week for one-third of a year. There are several voluntary Bible-classes among the students. The interest in the Bible among the students is decidedly increasing. The interest of college students in the study of the Bible may be stimulated by having it systematically taught by competent Bible scholars. The president would gladly aid in any effort to promote the systematic study of the Bible in the college or elsewhere."

President Gates, Amherst:

"Amherst College is one of the institutions which led the way in the systematic study in our colleges of the Bible, as a regular text-book.

Besides the four Bible-classes maintained and taught by members of the Faculty for the study of the Bible with reference to direct spiritual results, the Department of Biblical Literature is fully equipped and organized. This elective ranks in junior and senior year with the other electives in the course, and is chosen, by from ten to forty men in each class."

President Hyde, Bowdoin College:

"I am happy to say that one term of freshman year, four hours a week, is devoted to the study of one of the Gospels in Greek, as a basis for the study of a life of Christ. There are organized classes for the study of the Bible. I think the interest is on the increase. Have no suggestions to make, but we should be glad of help in this matter from any source."

President Eliot, Harvard:

"I do not think the Bible is used as a text-book, in the sense in which you use the word. In our Divinity School we have courses on the Old and New Testaments, Church History, Comparative Religion, Sociology, and Theology; all of which courses, with insignificant exceptions, can be counted toward the degree of Bachelor of Arts. The Divinity School is undenominational, no denomination having at this time more than one-third of the students. The Bible-classes for students are conducted by pastors of neighboring Churches in Cambridge, and are organized in the several religious societies of the university. As to the best way of promoting an interest in the study of the Bible, it is done here by maintaining stated interesting religious services in the university chapel every week-day morning, and every Sunday evening and Thursday afternoon during the winter, the attendance on which is wholly voluntary. I should not approve of using the English Bible as a text-book in ordinary weekly instruction in large heterogeneous classes. I think it has been abundantly demonstrated that it is not a good way to use the Bible.

The conditions here are somewhat peculiar, inasmuch as the university contains representatives of almost every possible religious belief; and no single denomination is represented by more than one-sixth of the whole number of students. The teachers, also, are of many denominations."

President Carter, Williamstown:

"The Bible is not used as a text-book in our institution; I can not say the interest in the Bible among our students is on the increase. There are organized Bible-classes, taught by the professors, but they are generally under the auspices of the Young Men's Christian Association. I can not suggest any method of increasing the interest in the Bible among college students. My belief is that there should be, in every college, elective courses in Bible study. We offer such a course every year; but the gentleman who conducts it required rather severe work of his class the first year, and the students have been shy of it ever since. Where the college is small and the religious sentiment and tradition is strong, I see no reason why the Bible should not be required as part of the curriculum. I should certainly be glad to see the study of the Bible everywhere increased. I do not know that your Society can do much, except to awaken a general interest in the subject."

President Warren, Boston University:

"Elective courses in Bible study are offered in connection with our College of Liberal Arts, more this year than ever before. The number electing them is not large, but perhaps never as large as now. A very high percentage of our students belong to the different evangelical Churches; but I do not know of any organized Bible-reading among them, except such as they carry on in their different Sunday-schools and Bible courses in the Churches where they worship."

President Chase, Bates College:

"We give one hour a week to a systematic Bible study by all the members of the freshman class. The work is laid out by the use of topical questions, requiring several hours' reading of the Bible itself, and of works dealing with Bible subjects. We spend an hour each week discussing the results obtained from the study. The interest in Bible study is decidedly on the increase. There are voluntary classes carried on under the auspices of the Young Men's and Young Women's Christian Associations. Our method is largely an attempt to show the relation of Bible history and teaching to the moral questions of our own time. Our Bible study is really the study of Christian ethics. We find our students greatly interested. Would be glad to be acquainted with the literature and methods of your Society. We use the International Sunday-school Lessons, and have frequent lectures on the Bible."

From Mount Holyoke College we have this response:

"The Bible is used as a text-book in our college. The time given is one hour a week for four years—144 hours in all; and it is required work. There are five organized Bible-reading classes among our students; also, three organized classes for mission study, which at present take the place of other Bible-classes. The interest in Bible study is on the increase. The best way of increasing the interest in Bible study is the use of the highest methods of instruction."

President Irvine, Wellesley:

"The Bible has been used as a text-book in this college ever since its opening. The present requirement is that of four hours out of the fifty-nine required for the Bachelor of Arts degree. Regularly organized classes for the study of the Bible have been formed by the students among their own numbers. Interest in Bible study among our students is certainly not declining. We think that the history of the Bible study in this college proves that such is generally interesting, when ably conducted. The friendly interest of your Society is, in itself, an encouragement and assistance."

On the whole, this report shows that the authorities of our colleges and universities are alive to the subject, and doing, each in his sphere, and according to his best judgment, what seems wisest in the premises. Certainly, the Bible is not ignored or totally neglected. There is a great advance upon the condition of things a generation ago; and the evident trend is toward more study of the Bible, if not toward putting the Bible into the regular curriculum.—*President Rankin, in the Independent.*

A LAUREATE'S DEBT TO THE BIBLE.

LORD TENNYSON'S debt to the Bible is one of the most striking incidents in the history of letters. It sustains Professor Huxley's admission that the Bible has been woven into all that is best in English literature. There are 460 quotations or allusions in the laureate's works—201 from the Old Testament, 259 from the New Testament. These quotations are from 52 out of the 66 books.

A PRAYER OVER THE BIBLE.

THE following prayer was prefixed to some editions of the early English versions of the Bible:

"O gracious God and most merciful Father, which hast vouchsafed us the rich and precious jewel of thy Holy Word, assist us by thy Spirit, that it may be written in our hearts; to our everlasting comfort, to reprove us, to renew us according to thine own image; to build us up, and edify us unto the perfect building of thy Christ; sanctifying and increasing in us all heavenly virtues. Grant this, O Heavenly Father, for Jesus Christ's sake. Amen."

www.ingramcontent.com/pod-product-compliance
Lightning Source LLC
Chambersburg PA
CBHW020824230426
43666CB00007B/1087